HYPNOTHERAPY MADE EASY

MASTERING THE ART OF NLP & HYPNOSIS

Based on an original format entitled:

"The Professional Art of Stage Hypnosis and Hypnotherapy"

Researched, Written and Devised by:

Jonathan Royle (Previously Alex LeRoy)
(D.Hyp) (D.NLP) (D.CMT) (D.SM) (D.CV) (D.SH) (D.Psy)

Special thanks to:

DELAVAR

As ex-President of The British Council of Professional Stage Hypnotists and tutor of some of the worlds leading stage performers and therapists including the author Jonathan Royle, Delavars help, advice and instruction has been invaluable in ensuring this course is the most comprehensive training course of its kind available anywhere.

Entire Course Copyright 2017 Jonathan Royle.

This course was first written in 1994 by Jonathan Royle.

ALL CORRESPONDENCE TO:

www.MagicalGuru.com and www.Magicalguru.co.uk

Introduction

Welcome to the mysterious world of hypnotherapy and related mind therapies. Allow me to introduce myself. My name is Jonathan Royle. I was born on the 13/08/75 into a show business family and made my stage debut aged three as Flap the Clown on Gandeys Circus (voted UK's no.1 circus show).

Since then I have gone from strength to strength, having been a full time professional performer for almost twenty years. During this time I've performed in many areas of show business from clowning and stand-up comedy, to fire-eating and illusions. Not to mention my other talents of comedy pick pocketing, five object juggling, tarot card reading, paper tearing, balloon modeling, mind reading and Pseudo clairvoyance shows and of course more recently adding Stage Hypnotism and Mind Therapies to my varied repertoire.

A MASTER OF ALL TRADES AND JACK OF NONE.

Since learning Hypnotherapy in 1989 and becoming a member of The Association of Professional Hypnotherapists and Psychotherapists, I have spent a large proportion of my time helping people with their fears, phobias and other emotional problems.

I've stopped hundreds of people from smoking, helped people to lose weight, gain confidence and to achieve numerous other things with great ease all of which has proven to me beyond doubt just how powerful Hypnosis is and can be as a Therapeutic tool. Along the way I've also lectured for psychology courses, run stress management classes for major household name blue chip companies and also run self-improvement seminars for the general public.

During 1993 I also had the pleasure of organising and promoting events featuring Mr. David Landau, who is highly respected within the world of Mind Therapies. These seminars and training days which I both helped to organise and promote were not only a great success but also gave me the chance of personal one to one instruction from David.

It was in November 1993 that I first got the idea to develop this course as on the 21st of November 93 I did a one-day training seminar. The seminar was sold out. Within two weeks of being advertised, the event, which was attended by hypnotherapists from all over England, all of whom had many years experience, received rave reviews in many of the leading hypnotherapy societies members only magazines. This indicated to me that there really was a lack of accurate and simple to understand information available in all areas of hypnosis and mind therapies and so the course was born.

Having been taught by some of the leading experts in the business and having had the luck to get my break so early into my hypnotism career, I have amassed a wealth of hands on performing and therapeutic experience from tutors who, in some cases have taken over 50 years to gather. I would hope now that you have confidence in me as your head tutor, as to benefit fully from what you will learn. You need to have faith in the skills that you learn and you can only have complete faith in these skills by first having faith in your teacher.

Nothing will be held back. This course will contain everything which is of value to a professional hypnotherapist. There follows, many pages, which explain in clear step by step detail all of the secrets, ploys and techniques that are used to become a safe and competent hypnotherapist.

These skills will enable you to enter this lucrative profession which can open new doors in your attitude and lifestyle that you never dreamed possible. I will introduce you to the profession of hypnotherapy and by so doing, initiate you into a profession which will fascinate and astound people including yourself.

To finish this introductory chapter, allow me to explain that this course has been purposely written in a simple to understand manner with plain language and complicated words and phrases removed. As closely to the way the majority of us speak. This has been established as the best possible way to learn, absorb and understand information which may be new and alien to us. Grammar and syntax will be thrown away in the interests of passing on the knowledge easily, quickly, enjoyably and effectively to you.

Hypnosis is a much deeper subject than most realize. The majority of the population is of the opinion that all you do is snap your fingers or swing a shiny watch in front of their eyes and then they will just instantly drop off to sleep. Well I can tell you here and now it is a great deal more complicated than that, yet at the same time if you are prepared to believe what I teach you it is also far easier to learn than you might at first imagine.

Born Plain Alex William Smith on the 13th August 1975 into a showbiz family, Royle made his stage debut aged 3 as Flap the Clown, later as Alex-Le-Roy he became Known as a Magician & Illusionist, Mind-Reader and Psychic Entertainer before becoming Internationally known as Jonathan Royle World Famous Hypnotist.

He started treating people Professionally with Hypnotherapy & NLP back in 1989 aged just 14.

His Hypnotic Stage Shows started Professionally in 1990 aged just 15.

His British National Television Debut as a Comedy Stage Hypnotist occurred in Jan 1993 aged 17.

His first Training Seminar teaching other Hypnotists was in September 1993 aged 18.

As Dr. Jonathan Royle Ph.D aka Lord Alex William Smith he has dozens of books available on Amazon and from all major book sellers covering all areas of NLP, Hypnotherapy. Stage-Hypnosis, Street Hypnotism, Magic, Mentalism, Self-Help and Marketing.

To date he is arguably responsible for the original training and/or ongoing mentoring and coaching of more people who are now Successful

Professional Comedy Stage Hypnotists and/or Hypnotherapy Practitioners all around the World than any other living Hypnosis trainer today.

His Home Study Training DVDS have been shipped to every Country in the World and he has also acted as a Hypnotic Consultant and Adviser to other Famous Name Stage-Hypnotists, Television Life Coaches, Celebrity Hypnotherapists and even Famous Name Masters of Mentalism Style Mind Control.

He has been featured using his "Mind Skills" on major name celebrities on TV & Radio Shows around the World as well as regualrly being featured in National & International Newspapers and Magazines.

The story about the Lady whose fear of traffic wardens he cured appeared on the Full Front Page along with a double page feature inside "The Sun" which was Britain's biggest read newspaper when the story appeared in the mid 90's.

He was the only British Hypnotherapist to be chosen for and then featured in a therapeutic interaction with Robert De Niro and Billy Crystal to help promote their 2002 Film "Analyse That" - This feature first appeared in Amercias largest Circulated newspaper "USA Today" and was then syndicated to publications all over the World.

Royle is the President of The Association of Complete Mind Therapists (ACMT) which incorporates The Association of Professional Hypnotherapists & Psychotherapists (APHP)

He is also the President of The Professional Organisation of Stage Hypnotists (POSH) which incorporates The Association of Professional Stage Hypnotists (APSH)

Years ago he created his own unique one session treatment approach of "Complete Mind Therapy" - (CMT) which is now used by therapists across the globe to help people overcome their Habits, Addictions, Fears, Phobias and most other things you can possibly think of from A through to Z in a single 45 to 90 minute treatment session.

Whilst in more recent years he has devised "Mind Emotion Liberation Techniques" - (M.E.L.T) which helps you to M.E.L.T. your clients problems away in a matter of minutes...

And most recently of all he has just started training others in "Complete Unconscious Reprogramming of Emotional Disease & Distress (C.U.R.E.D) which enables you to give your clients the C.U.R.E (Complete Unconscious Reprogramming of Emotions) for their issues.

His work and innovations in the field of Hypnosis has led to him becoming only the Fourth Hypnotist in History to date (August 2017) to have ever been inducted into the South African Academy of Hypnotists "HYPNOTISTS HALL OF FAME" as per this info:

https://klearthoughtsmentalismhypnosis.wordpress.com/2016/08/26/hypnosis-hall-of-fame-excellence-award-for-rochdale-greater-manchester-england-hypnotist-jonathan-royle-the-king-of-hypnotherapy-nlp-hypnotism-trainers/

Back when Paul McKenna ran a Company with Michael Breen called McKenna Breen Ltd in London, Paul advised the majority of his staff and also seminar supervisors to study Royle's "MindCare Organisation" Home Study Course on Hypnotherapy & Stage-Hypnosis and indeed many of them did exactly that.

When organising The International Hypnosis Conference in London, Valerie Austin invited Royle along as a Guest and his inclusion on the discussion panel was indeed a major talking point amongst those who attended.

When John Cerbone & Richard Nongard came to Manchester England to run one of their "Speed Trance" events, Royle was invited along to act as an Adviser and Consultant on British Stage Hypnosis & Street Hypnotism Laws.

Amercian Hypnotist & Internet Entrepreneur Tellman Knudson engaged Royle to speak on what was at the time (and may well still be) the Worlds Biggest Ever Online Hypnotherapy Training Event "The Hypnosis Event" and also engaged him to take part in what was at the time the World's Biggest Ever Online NLP Training Event "The NLP Event"

British NLP & Hypnotic Marketing Expert James Lavers aka "The Lazy Coach" sought to interview Royle and this was one of the most positively raved about sections of his "NLP Masters of Passive Income" Study Package.

Leading UK NLP Expert, Authour of "The Rainbow Machine" and founder of Integrral Eye Movement Therapy booked Royle to speak for his NLP Meet up group and afterwards he said:

"Undoubtedly one of the funniest, most intelligent and hugely entertaining presentations on hypnosis, NLP and therapy I have experienced. Go and see Jonathan – he will rock your beliefs, make you laugh out loud and probably outrage you. The hypnosis and NLP world needs more people like him. Jonathan Royle – APPROVED!"
ANDREW T. AUSTIN – CHICHESTER – Nov. 2005

He was also invited by "The Incredible Hypnotist" Richard Barker to be the First Ever Headline Speaker on the First Ever "Hypnotist Entertainment Cruise" and for this he received rave reviews from all who attended.

His Hypnosis training Seminars have SOLD OUT in Las Vegas (organised by Jay Noblezada) - California (Organised by Brian Stracner) and in many other locations around the World.

His October 2017 "The Royle Event" one day training as organised and promoted by Television "Fat Families" Presenter and Clinical Hypnotherapist Steve Miller SOLD OUT in less than a week of the tickets being placed onto sale.

His Home Study Courses, Training Books and Live Events have received rave reviews from experts all over the world as can be seen in the numerous video testimonials at this link:

https://klearthoughtsmentalismhypnosis.wordpress.com/2015/01/09/what-the-experts-say-about-jonathan-royles-hypnotherapy-nlp-stage-and-street-hypnosis-and-mentalism-and-marketing-training-courses/

Recently he was made an Honorary Life member of The United Kingdom Board of Clinical Hypnotherapy - (UKBCH) who have also approved and endorsed his various training courses and materials.

Indeed his training courses and materials are also Approved, Endorsed and/or Accredited by:

*The MindCare Organisation Ltd - UK

*Personal Development Associates - USA

*The Neuro Linguistic Programming Practitioners Association - (NLPPA) - UK

*The Royle Institute of Hypnotherapy & Psychotherapy - (RIHP)

He is considered by many to be the Most Controversial, Outspoken & Daringly Honest Hypnotist of all time and this has led to rumours galore and defamatory lies circulating all over the internet.

The REAL TRUTH behind the negative stuff you may have seen posted can be seen (with evidence) at this link:

http://www.drjonathanroyle-awarning-exposed.com/

And the REAL TRUTH (with evidence) behind how he was also once Britain's Biggest Ever Media Prankster and back in 1998 attempted to expose the dishonest & criminal actions of the now Jailed & Disgraced Rupert Murdoch Journalist The "Fake Sheikh" Mazher Mahmood can be seen at this link:

https://klearthoughtsmentalismhypnosis.wordpress.com/2013/10/19/the-naked-truth-about-dr-jonathan-royle-aka-alex-william-smith-aka-alex-leroy-hypnotist-magician-and-psychic-entertainer/

His Official Website is at **http://www.magicalguru.com/** and his online store is at **http://www.magicalguru.co.uk/**

For those who like the Comedy Stage Hypnosis side of things there are tons of clips from Royle's Hypnotist Shows taken from events around the World over the past 25+ years on his Youtube Channel "CelebrityHypnotist" at these links:

https://www.youtube.com/playlist?list=PLK4pimF35bjhUcUfdlgKSM k6SK_I2u2f8

And also at this link there are even more clips…

https://www.youtube.com/playlist?list=PLDhI8Pk4O_4DXXiDg53V6 UzOSJrF1avxf

Or Go to the You-Tube Channel of ***www.youtube.com/CelebrityHypnotist/***

Read, study and absorb the contents of this course, it will without doubt place you on the road to ultimate success in hypnotherapy. I wish you luck in your future career, although if you absorb the contents of this course which is filled with liquid gold knowledge then your success is almost guaranteed.

<u>**PART ONE**</u>

The Key Points

"Scientists say that we only use 10% of our brain power, well in that case what do we do with the other 47%?"

Seriously though, the potential of the human mind is literally unlimited and far greater than the average person could ever imagine. As you will discover in this chapter the key secret to hypnosis is the belief and expectancy within your subjects mind, may the general public remain ignorant to the way their minds work otherwise we hypnotists will be out of business!

In this part I will reveal all the key secrets of Hypnosis. In other words, within the next few pages you will find everything you require to become a professional mind therapist like myself or Paul McKenna.   However as you will have, I presume, no previous knowledge of the subjects in hand you may think that the next few pages over simplify the art. The idea of this however is to show you the key points and then to explain to you why these are the key points. As such when you have read the last part of this course you will then realise and more importantly understand just how easy and simple it really is to hypnotise someone.

So this is if you like what most people would have made the last chapter of this course, but for reasons you will understand later, it has been presented "Back to front!" The main advantage of doing it this way is that you will learn both the cause of what you are doing and also the effect it has upon people. This will mean that you will automatically know more than a great number of hypnotherapists. Always remember <u>EVERY CAUSE HAS AN EFFECT</u> and <u>EVERY EFFECT HAS A UNDERLYING CAUSE.</u>

THE KEYS TO HYPNOTIC INDUCTIONS

When wishing to place someone into a Hypnotic trance there is a set procedure to follow which is:

A) BELIEF and EXPECTANCY

B) DISORIENTATION and CONFUSION
C) SUGGESTION and REPETITION
D) RELAXATION and SLEEP

Step A means that if you instill into them a belief in your powers as a Hypnotist and as such they believe that you are able to place them under trance, and they also expect to go under if you were to try it upon them, then they are in the correct state of mind to be very successfully and rapidly placed into a Hypnotic trance state.

Step B means that once they are in the correct state of mind to be Hypnotised you then use methods of disorientation and confusion to convince them they are starting to go into trance, and that's why they are feeling these strange effects. As such if they believe this to be the case then they will expect to go under deeper and as such they will, as in the end it's all down to their personal state of mind.

Step C means that once these things are starting to convince them they are beginning to slip into trance then you use methods of suggestion and repetition to confuse and disorientate them even further and also to convince them that they are going under more. If they believe this is the case and expect what you are doing to have an effect upon them, then indeed, in turn it most certainly will.

Step D is the end result of carrying out steps A, B & C and should be that if they believe what you have done to be Hypnosis and expect it to work then this will have the result of relaxation and sleep. And as all Hypnosis really is, is deep relaxation they will then be in the Hypnotic trance state.

So you see the secret to all induction's of any kind whether Stage or Therapy and whether slow, rapid or instantaneous is that if the subject sincerely believes that what you are doing does work and they also sincerely believe and expect it to work on them, then the end result will always be that it works on them. Basically, the key secret to all inductions is to have instilled into the prospective subjects mind, the belief in your powers and the 100% expectancy that they will be hypnotised.

<u>BELIEF AND EXPECTANCY EQUALS HYPNOSIS.</u>

THE THREE STEPS TO HYPNOSIS

An even simpler way to explain how Hypnosis works to place someone into a trance state is like this:

A. They must know that you are a Professional Hypnotist and can therefore do as you claim.
B. Ask them to close their eyes and to breathe deeply and regularly.
C. Suggest ideas of heaviness, sleep, tiredness and relaxation to them for a few minutes and then THEY WILL BE IN A HYPNOTIC TRANCE.

Once again I'm sure you can see how it all relates back to those two key words/secrets which of course are belief and expectancy.

PEOPLE HYPNOTISE THEMSELVES

The hypnotist only tells them that they can do it! Until he told them, they never knew that they could do it. In effect we are "directors" of the film and the clients become the "actors" doing as we say. We just guide them into what is really just a deep state of relaxation and should really be classed as "Self Hypnosis".

THE PLACEBO EFFECT.

One important thing that applies only to therapeutic work is that of the placebo effect. By the time your client has read your newspaper advertisement and/or been given a personal recommendation about you by a previous client, belief and expectancy are already going to work on their minds. It then takes a lot of courage to phone you and book an appointment for therapy as this is then a conscious decision within themselves that things must change and will change for the better. The prospect of attending at your house or office is one that will fill them with much apprehension and this is why in some cases, clients will not show up for their appointments as the thought of change becomes just too scary. However when a client does show up as happens in 99% of the cases they are almost cured of their problem the moment they step into your consulting room, as they have already made a conscious decision by booking the appointment and attending on time that things must change!

The other piece in the jigsaw is when you get them to hand over the payment for the session before you even start the Therapy. Most people do not like parting with money, especially not large amounts of it, such as the fee of around £40 per hour, which you will be charging them for your time and as such paying this fee makes them believe in your abilities to help them even more. The final 25% of the therapeutic process is the actual treatment which you give them, although even if this were to be fundamentally worthless (which it is not), if the client is made to believe it will be beneficial then indeed it will!

GOLDEN RULES TO FOLLOW

RULE ONE: Have total confidence in yourself and your skilful abilities.

RULE TWO: Exude that confidence so that others will then have total confidence in you and your abilities.

RULE THREE: Monotony and repetition is the trade of the Hypnotist so repeat, repeat and then repeat it again.

RULE FOUR: Learn to use your voice so that it can sound demanding and also commanding.

RULE FIVE: Follow the steps and instructions detailed within this course to the letter and your success is guaranteed.

YOUR HYPNOTIC TOOLKIT

As a Hypnotist, the only tools of use to you are self-confidence (which you must have in abundance), suggestion, commanding and demanding tone of voice, rhythm of speech (cadence), monotony, repetition, professional appearance, knowledge and experience. These are the only tools available to you. However, if you learn to use them all effectively then it will become a most powerful tool kit and will make your job far easier. So learn to handle these tools with finesse for they are the start, middle and end of all that you must do and know.

SOME OTHER MOST IMPORTANT POINTS

1. Hypnotists are not Hypnotists, they are merely actors playing the part of the image of a Hypnotist which people expect to see and as such react to.

2. All Hypnosis whether is really just self hypnosis.

3. Hypnosis occurs due to co-operation and not confrontation or challenge.

4. As Hypnosis is just a state of mind and compliance based on the clients levels of belief and expectancy, there is no such thing as a "Hypnotised" feeling and this is because each person experiences everything that happens during the course of their life differently.

5. Belief and expectancy are the most powerful keys of all to success.

6. Suggestion correctly expressed is Hypnosis.

7. The correct way to express suggestion is in a commanding and demanding voice, and to keep on repeating it to the subject.

8. For suggestions of sleep, slow deep tones of voice with words suggesting a downward motion are used.

9. For awakening suggestions, a faster, higher tone of voice with words suggesting an upward motion would be used.

10. The salesmen's techniques of mirroring and matching are used to put people to ease, make them relax and to establish rapport easily.

11. Hypnosis is a state of heightened awareness and as such clients can taste, smell, see, feel and hear things better than they usually would be able and are more, rather than less aware of their surroundings.

12. If the mind is focused on one thing or at least one thing at a time and is

not allowed to wander, then as the normal worries of the day are not considered your client will automatically relax completely. When people relax they tend to lose a lot of their inhibitions.

13. Confidence begets confidence and as a man thinketh so he becomes, which proves that positive thinking is a most positive force.

14. It has to be in the mind first before it becomes an action (in every day life) and it has to be in the subconscious mind first to become an action during Hypnosis.

15. When the imagination (subconscious mind) and the will (conscious mind) are in conflict, the imagination always wins. So if you can get a person to focus their mind on something to the exclusion of everything else, you are then able to bypass the critical area of their minds and firmly embed a suggestion into their imagination without any conscious conflict! Then afterwards even if the conscious mind were to try and oppose the suggestion the far stronger force of the imagination would always win and the suggestion would be acted upon.

16. Hypnosis merely shuts down the analytical (critical) area of the mind that is located between the conscious and subconscious. It acts as a kind of "gate-keeper" and processes all incoming information from the conscious mind before it is allowed to enter the subconscious mind where it is permanently kept on file.

17. As we've already stated if the suggestion can be given directly to the subconscious mind (the imagination) then it will be acted upon immediately and as I've stated already all Hypnosis does is shut down that analytical (critical) area of the mind which in turn makes this action possible.

18. Talk success, think success, act success and dream success and then successful things will occur.

19. Remember positive thoughts breed positive actions. They are contagious and positive actions breed positive results.

20. Relaxation is the key, which opens the door to the subconscious mind.

In this state, get the client to visualise your suggestions with implicit faith that it is so and so and it will be.

21. Co-operations with a highly developed imagination are the best qualities your client can have for successful acceptance of your Hypnotic suggestions.

22. You want your clients to have confidence, belief and faith with expectation of success, but it is no use just telling them this. They must be "sold" on Hypnosis and its effects to possess these real qualities.

23. Rapport, observation, recognition and leadership. These are the four stages of inducing a Hypnotic trance. All are lead by the client and merely followed by the Hypnotist as will be explained later. Rapport should establish three things, trust, comfort and of course belief.

24. Hypnosis is merely a form of communication. Tone of voice is essential in all communication and indeed in Hypnosis also. It is also possible to hide "secret" messages within a spoken sentence by changing your tone of voice so that they have an almost "subliminal" effect.

25. If they believe that you have special powers then your job is easy, if they expect to be hypnotised by you then they will be! They are in a strange situation whereas you feel at ease. You make them feel important, needed and appreciated whilst also conditioning them so that they sincerely believe they are only clever and intelligent if they co-operate with you.

26. You know what's going to happen and they don't so you are already ahead of them. You act in a routine manner as though it always works and it will then work.

27. Always paint a verbal picture, so that the clients know what is expected of them. They must know what you are saying as they cannot read your mind. The suggestions you give must also have one meaning only so that they cannot be misinterpreted.

28. You must take the consulting room over. Show that you and you alone

are in charge. Demand instant respect, dominate your clients. Give them orders and expect them to be obeyed, talk and act in an authoritative manner and look at ease with all you do. Keep their mind off what's happening at all times and then you'll be well on your way to Hypnotic success.

Lastly for this part, allow me to explain how Hypnosis works between the subject and the Hypnotist in much the same way as a Bio-feedback machine. Also let me explain briefly how the human mind works, we'll elaborate later on.

THE HUMAN MIND AS I SEE IT

As I see it the human mind is made up of three separate layers making the whole, these three layers are as follows:

1) The conscious mind and/or human will.
2) The analytical and/or critical area.
3) The subconscious and/or imagination

We use the conscious mind to speak etc, the subconscious deals with the automatic actions of our blood circulation and breathing as well as being our imagination area of the mind. And lastly the analytical area analyses all incoming information before being allowed entry and storage in the subconscious mind as truth/fact.

I will now make the analogy of the mind being a computer. The conscious mind is if you like the keyboard, which inputs new information. The analytical area analyses it for any mistakes in much the same way as a spell checker, then the "corrected" data, if of an acceptable nature, is allowed to enter the subconscious mind where it is stored forever in much the same way as storing data onto a floppy disc.

To briefly explain in terms of stage hypnosis; if you told a fully conscious person that when you snapped your fingers they are Elvis and then snapped same said fingers, they would not react! Why? Well simply because the analytical area processes it and then compares it with the memory bank record in the subject's subconscious mind of who they are before rejecting it as it realises the statement to be untrue. All this of course takes only a fraction of a second to occur.

Under Hypnosis the mind and body of the subject relax, and due to the disorientation, confusion and repetition of suggestion the analytical area shuts down or goes to sleep. As such when told that on a snap of the fingers they will be Elvis the mind is then unable to process the information and find out that it is untrue and consequently it is believed to be true. It goes directly into the subconscious as being true and so is acted upon as an automatic reflex action.

If only in a very light state of trance the will of the person may still go into conflict with the imagination or subconscious, but as we stated earlier when the imagination and will are in conflict the imagination always wins. As such they will react and be Elvis or do whatever you have suggested without question.

This part contains all the keys you require for Hypnotic success, but I'll end by explaining how the mind is like a Bio-feedback machine. Observe Figure A and you will see the Hypnotist facing a person. The final key to a most successful induction is as follows. The Hypnotist suggests things to the subject who in turn accepts and reacts to these verbal suggestions. The Hypnotist then observes the effects of those suggestions and feeds back his observations as new suggestions to the subject. The person accepts and reacts to these, the Hypnotist observes the effects and then feeds back the observations as new suggestions to the client and so the Biofeedback computer effect continues until the clientt is in a deep state of trance. In other words the Hypnotist's suggestions are always made up of his observations.

FIGURE A

THE BIOFEEDBACK COMPUTER EFFECT

An example of this so that you fully understand how it works would be as follows. The Hypnotist suggests that the client will start to breathe deeply and regularly, this is then accepted by the client and acted upon by them. They then start to breathe more deeply and regularly and perhaps also start to close their eyes. The Hypnotist observes this and then feeds back the observation to the subject as new suggestions along the line of "That's great and as you continue to breathe deeply and regularly, notice how your eyelids are now so heavy and so tired, in fact it's so much easier, just to let them close!" The client accepts and reacts, the Hypnotist observes and feeds back the observations as new suggestions and so the cycle continues.

This now means that you really do know how to hypnotise someone, as with this technique the wording of your induction must always be ad lib and worded so as to contain your observations and as such capitalise upon them. You would of course at all times be following the basic guidelines of voice tone and speed of suggestions etc. And remember the key words associated by most people with Hypnosis and a trance state are: sleep, relax, drifting, deeper, falling, resting, calm, heavy, tired and all other words associated which mean similar things to these.

Well congratulations you now know more about hypnosis than most if not all of the "cowboy" hypnotists who are currently flooding the industry. You will have noticed by now I'm sure, that throughout this course, I will repeat many key points several times, the reason for this is that the trade of any Hypnotist is repetition and you can only learn through repetition. As such, this course has been written, not only to be enjoyable to read, but rather in a way that you learn the maximum amount possible in the shortest space of time possible.

PART TWO

WHAT IS HYPNOSIS?

Derived from the Greek word "Hypnos" meaning sleep, Hypnosis is seen as being a power when in fact it is, as the Oxford English Dictionary says. "A form of communication where suggestions can be given most effectively by one person to then be carried out be the receiver of those suggestions." The answer I give when asked this question of what is hypnosis? Is the one which I learnt from Delavar's training manual "The Hypnotists Bible" and it goes like this:

Hypnosis is that small moment in time when the Ego gives way to the I.D. and vice versa. With hypnosis, we can extend that fraction of a nano second into a period of time as long as we like. We are then at this time in communication with both the Ego and the Id. We have the Ego, that is you (when awake) and the I.D. (you when asleep). To clarify further, the I.D. controls your body all the time but has no control over the Ego, whereas the Ego has no real control over the body, only the emotions are affected by it. You breathe, think, taste, smell, feel pain, keep your heart beating and so on only because the I.D. is there to see to it! The Ego is the part, which makes you walk down the street with a swagger because you feel you are the best thing since sex was invented. It is also your Ego that allows you to go on stage as the world's No.1 hypnotist or invite clients into your consulting room. We need both the Ego and the I.D. However they cannot both be in charge at the same time, so we say the Ego when awake and the I.D. when asleep. OK so this is true but what is hypnosis? Well the I.D. can always overrule the Ego, Ego awake and I.D. when asleep. So this then really is an explanation of what hypnosis is or what happens when it occurs.

Now there comes a time twice a day (normally) when the Ego and the I.D. need to communicate with each other, can you remember going to sleep? Can you remember waking up? (Nobody can!) Before you go to sleep or awaken there is a transitional period of a few seconds. That period is the time when the Ego and the I.D. give instructions to each other, the only time when they can if you like come together. To get to this period, we always dream, we drift off to sleep and awaken with a dream also (It acts as a distraction for the mind as in the hypnotic induction process). It is this transitional period when the Ego and the I.D. are exchanging dominant positions and it momentarily confuses the brain function. This is what the hypnotist uses and his induction methods if you like, merely extending this transitional period from a few seconds into very long periods of time and it is this we now call the hypnotic state.

A few extra points on the side, under hypnosis (deep relaxation) the I.D. can take full control of all the bodily functions, but the Ego is still in a watchful state as it never likes to give up full control. During sleep of a normal kind, the I.D. has a free hand to repair some of the damage caused by the uncaring Ego. In a hypnotic trance we do not cut off the supply of Oxygen to the brain as happens in normal sleep, we do in fact go straight to the dividing line between the Ego and the I.D. so that the subject is neither awake nor asleep. They are in that mid point between the two points/states. It's this midpoint which is hypnosis. In layman's terms I will now explain how this state (in trance) feels and also what its like/what it is.

WHAT IS A TRANCE STATE?

Nobody really knows, there are many theories, however in scientific terms a trance is measurable by changes in brain activity and behaviour. Auto-suggestion, Yoga, meditation and self-hypnosis all induce a trance state. The reason why the trance state is so hard to understand is because they are so commonplace that it is hard to tell when you are in one or not. The closest I can come to an explanation of a trance state is the state in which the mind selects what it is consciously going to pay attention to. For example when you are watching a Western on TV, you are not sitting in your living room observing an electronic device, you have suspended disbelief and if it is a good film for long periods of time you will feel that you are actually in Dodge City observing those gunslingers in action! You are ignoring the sound of the traffic outside your window because it is not part of the story, you are unaware that you leg has gone to sleep or that the dog has just chewed its way through the newspaper, this then is a trance state.

A Boxer is hit many times during a bout but only the really hard blows hurt. All the little jabs and ineffective punches that would under normal conditions hurt the boxer as much as you and I go by unnoticed. The Boxer is concentrating on his opponent's moves and actions to the exclusion of all else, even pain! This too is a trance state.

Another example is a good driver, one who does not consciously think about the physical act of driving, changing gear, moving pedals and so on, but instead concentrates on the road ahead and the other drivers around them. He/She has turned the driving over to the subconscious and this too is a trance state.

When so engrossed in a book that you don't even hear a person's offer of a drink, this too is yet another example of a trance state. All of these examples are trance states and all of them are normal and safe. If the adverts come on whilst watching TV, the bell goes off during the boxing match, or the car engine makes a funny noise whilst driving, you simply change your focus of attention from the trance state to the new scenario. You are in fact fully aware and awake at all times, just as the hypnotic subjects on stage and/or in therapy are. You are under nobodies "control" but your own, you have not become deaf or had any of your senses dulled and above all the transition is so quick that it goes by unnoticed. I'm sure you will have experienced many such examples in your life in the past and so you see you already know from personal experience what a trance state is and what it feels like to be in one.

In the hypnotic trance state you can still be fully aware of your surroundings and situation, the only real difference is that you are no longer in control of the switch which operates the normal automatic control systems. You have willingly and happily given this power to another. Many people who have been hypnotised, especially those who have only been under a low key influence, for example like when being told to stop smoking, will feel that they have been tricked because they have not yet lost full consciousness. If only they knew that hypnosis is a state of heightened awareness.

This feeling of having been tricked is due to their own misconceptions and preconceived ideas of what hypnosis is all about. They often complain to their friends "What a rip off the whole thing was" yet they never again touch another cigarette.

One way to imagine how the mind works is to imagine it as an art gallery full of beautiful pictures. As a person is walking through it, the gallery is the subconscious mind and the person the conscious. As the person looks upon a picture, he is all absorbed by its beauty and form, but all the other pictures are still there. They are just not being paid attention to at this time. If you think of the conscious mind as the real you (your personality), the part of your mind that thinks in language, then you are misleading yourself. You are in fact far more complex that that! Let us imagine what you are doing right now whilst reading this course. First your eyes are scanning the page and the meaning of the words are coming into your brain. You are not consciously thinking A is for apple, N is for nightie, D is for daisy and so on, instead you just read the word AND. These other things were committed to your subconscious mind and became conditioned into you so that they now work as an automatic reflex action and all this was learnt as a child. What happened is your conscious mind decided to sit and read the course and to open a channel to your subconscious mind, to the bit in the "computer file" marked "reading and how to do it". This in itself is a trance state (a distraction of the conscious mind) which your conscious mind was in until I alerted you to the situation.

Also until I alerted you to the situation, your conscious mind was lost amongst all these new ideas that I am sharing with you. Therefore you are not thinking about the gas bill or next Sunday's weather, you have not either considered your surroundings at all or the fact that you may be standing or sitting. It could in fact be argued in a very real sense, that I have hypnotised you or induced a trance state into you without us even meeting in person, for what has just been described is the essence of the hypnotic induction process.

One person's control of another's conscious mind by keeping it occupied with but one thought. That is what hypnosis is, not all that frightening now is it?

During hypnosis, it is the belief system and processes which must be overruled and controlled. Now the only way one person can control another persons belief mechanism is to bypass it completely and that is what hypnosis enables us to achieve. This is what allows us to convince subjects they are Elvis or Madonna. Because the belief system is not being consulted, it does not realise the discrepancy with fact and as such is not objecting to the command, as would usually be the case. If the belief mechanism were to check with the subconscious, it would find that it has been temporarily reprogrammed. The hypnotist bypasses the belief and understanding systems (reality safeguards) in the mind of another and influences the subconscious mind directly.

This is hypnosis at its simplest form. Just as when counting sheep in your mind at night to promote sleep, the distraction of the swinging watch or flashing light or moving hand is used to concentrate the mind of the client away from defensive so that they relax. Once they have relaxed, the hypnotist's words will seep more easily into the subconscious where they will then be enacted. Basically speaking, hypnosis is easy to achieve through fixation of attention and distraction of the client's mind away from what they are doing. It is the thinking behind the words you say and the flexibility and ingenuity you have as a hypnotist that matters.

In reality, hypnosis occurs due to a persons belief and expectancy and as we mentioned earlier the best kept secret of all is that all hypnosis is really just self-hypnosis, with us just acting as directors of the trance state. Now its time for a very brief history lesson:

Hypnosis is a condition in which willpower and a person's consciousness is suspended but other functions remain unimpaired. The subject of hypnosis is then exceptionally suggestible to suggestion, may be made insensible to pain and will carry out instructions (post hypnotic suggestions) at once or long after being awakened from the trance. Discovered by Anton Fredrich Mesmer (1733-1815), an Austrian physician who claimed he could reduce people to a trance like state by applying a technique he called Animal Magnetism. The subject's willpower being entirely subordinated by his own.

The police expelled him from Vienna and he created a sensation with stage and public demonstrations when he moved to Paris in 1778. But again in 1785 he was denounced as a charlatan despite his obvious powers. He was really just an early experimenter in what we now call hypnotism or hypnosis. It was however at the time called Mesmerism and was called this for many years afterwards also.

A surgeon by the name of James Esdaile Braid then, many years on, studied Mesmer's work and coined the name hypnosis from the Greek word Hypnos meaning sleep and so a whole new life was given to the suggestion technique. James E. Braid performed operations with only hypnosis as the anaesthetic and brought it as a science almost to the attention of the medical profession.

Another key peg in the development of hypnosis and its use in medicine and psychotherapy was Milton Erikson who's great books are available on general sale and publications authored by, or co-authored by this man are unreservedly recommended to all students of this course. From a stage performance point of view it was Peter Casson who made stage hypnosis so popular back in the 50's although obviously many Music Hall performers had been doing it for many years prior to this. It was due to Mr. Casson that the 1952 Hypnotism act was implemented, otherwise stage hypnotism shows may have been banned completely in England in 1952 no thanks to the actions of an American hypnotist called Ralph Slater who brought the industry into disrepute and for this we have a lot to thank Peter Casson for.

In more recent years there have been people such as Paul McKenna, Andrew Newton, Ken Webster, Peter Powers and myself presenting hypnosis on TV to millions of people at one time, bringing it to a much wider audience and so making hypnosis more popular than ever.

So all in all, its roots are set many years ago and it's an art that is tried, tested and proven to work. Well let me rephrase that. Hypnosis is a skill anyone can learn, but the practice of it is an art which can only be learnt through practical experience. Just as anyone can play a piano this does not automatically make them a great concert pianist and in the same way it follows that each and every hypnotist will have a different level of skill and only those with the highest skill levels could be classed as the concert pianists of stage hypnotism.

Hypnotism is a form of power over people, and any power when misused can be dangerous. This knowledge, like any other knowledge is given in trust to you, to be looked after, used for the good of all and shared with other like-minded people. Most importantly let me state that nobody has ever come to any harm under hypnosis or as a direct/indirect result of it despite what may have been said in the media (during 1993/1994) about the tragic death of one Sharon Tabarn, the daughter of Margaret Harper some five hours after a stage hypnotism show conducted by Andrew Vincent at the Roebuck Public house in Leyland (Preston) Lancs. Despite the fact that several people including her family and so called experts who should have known better, including top Hypnotherapist Derek Crussal, backed up Mrs. Harper's allegations of death by hypnosis and formed (C.A.S.H) The Campaign Against Stage Hypnotists she did in fact die due to natural causes.

Well the real truth as I understand it and it has been related to me is as follows. The coroners report, the pathologists report and all other expert reports concluded that her death was due to natural causes and has no connection whatsoever to the hypnotism show or the hypnotic trance state. In fact I am led to believe by what I have recently heard that excessive traces of alcohol and chemicals (not just prolactin) were found in her bloodstream and it is now generally believed within the industry that this is why she died tragically in her sleep by choking on her own vomit. So despite the false impression given by the mass media there was no connection whatsoever between hypnosis and the death of Sharon Tabarn and in fact there is no recorded case in history backed up with proper facts and evidence of anyone ever dying due to hypnosis.

Always remember that hypnosis is a totally harmless state (be is on stage or in the consulting room), which is why as detailed earlier, it is a natural part of our everyday lives. Hypnotism is the effect of the thoughts, feelings, imagination and will of each particular client. When the client's mind is in agreement with the mind of the hypnotist, according to a given suggestion, then this is hypnosis.

Take a look in your dictionary and the definition of hypnosis will no doubt mention sleep, it is a sleep like state, a trance if you like, in which the condition of the subject becomes passive and the subconscious mind accepts the hypnotists suggestions, providing of course that these fall within their moral code. Very briefly put, hypnotism is a psychological method of selling an idea by an operator (the hypnotist) to a subject under certain conditions. These conditions can be divided under two headings:

    1) Conditions applying to the operator (hypnotist).
    2) Conditions applying to the subject

It is also interesting to note that it is now an accepted fact that a subject under the influence of hypnotism will only carry out the hypnotist's requests when they are not against their morals or internal beliefs. This is not, to be honest, strictly true as in fact once a person has given their consent to be hypnotised and is under hypnosis they can be made to do anything you wish just so long as the suggestion is phrased correctly. By correctly, I mean worded so that to the subject it appears that they will be carrying out a perfectly pleasant act which ties in with their morals, but which has the end result of them doing as you wish.

You should by now, realise that when a person enters hypnosis, although they may themselves not believe this to be the case, (remember belief and expectancy) they are in fact going under by means of their own free will. They co-operate with you the hypnotist, to bring about this state of mind which is actually self-hypnosis.

POSITIVE THINKING IS A MOST POSITIVE FORCE

AND

CONFIDENCE BEGETS CONFIDENCE

From your point of view, the key secret of hypnosis is the faith in your abilities is the means and confidence is the weapon of execution.

IT HAS GOT TO BE IN THE MIND FIRST BEFORE IT CAN BECOME AN ACTION LATER

So quite simply, make sure all the suggestions you give are clear so that they do go into the mind first and then become actions late. Another important point is to always be enthusiastic in whatever you are doing then you will automatically become more successful as a result.

ENTHUSIASM IS ESSENTIAL - A NEVER TIRING ENTHUSIASM

Now, so that any fear of failure you may still have can be forgotten, allow me to state what is a very true fact indeed and that is:

Anyone can, if they so desire, become a competent professional hypnotherapist. The only quality which is 100% necessary is confidence and the ability to force ones own personality onto others. The only difference between you and the majority of people on planet earth is that you have, I assume a desire to practice the art of hypnotherapy and also an inner belief that you can do it! You should by now have the self confidence that by the end of this course you will be able to, without doubt become a hypnotherapist. Basically speaking all hypnotic inductions and trance deepening's have the following characteristics:

A) The client's attention and concentration is focused upon one stimulus or a range of limited stimuli. You can ask the client to gaze at a bright light or at a spot on the wall or ceiling, at the tip of your finger or indeed at their clasped hands. The client could even be just concentrating on the sound of the hypnotist's voice or the regular beat of a metronome. The client can focus upon feelings in their body or the ebb and flow of their own breath to mention just a few possible examples. The key secret here is to have the client focused and concentrated upon one thing and make it seem important at all times.

B) The hypnotist repeats continuously, suggestions of relaxation, letting go, sleep, heaviness, calmness, going down deeper and deeper etc.

C) The coupling of A & B combined, e.g. focusing their attention by a suggestion. For example, with each breath you take you are letting go more and more, as your eyes are getting heavier and heavier you find yourself drifting down deeper and deeper, or, each time your hands shake more rapidly, so in turn you drift deeper and deeper to sleep. These are all good examples of how to do this.

These three key points are present in one form or another in all the induction and deepening methods that you will ever encounter or indeed will ever use. Remember that the power of hypnosis does not lie within the hypnotist, but rather the real power is within the minds of the clients. The hypnotist just utilises the simple techniques within this course to unlock that power, and here I refer once more to the principle of belief and expectancy within the client's mind.

<u>**PART THREE**</u>

RAPPORT, OBSERVATION, RECOGNITION AND LEADERSHIP!

You have been offered the knowledge and wisdom required to act upon the opportunity to profit from being a hypnotherapist! But as Sir Winston Churchill so rightly said and I quote:

"Most people will at some time in their life stumble over opportunity. Unfortunately for them, most will just pick themselves up, dust themselves off and carry on as if nothing had ever happened."

Hi, welcome back again! Well let's deal in this chapter with rapport, observation, recognition and leadership. These are the four stages of inducing a hypnotic trance state. All are lead by the client and merely followed by you the hypnotist. I shall take each step one at a time and lead you through the techniques involved. However never forget that there is no substitute for practice and practical application! And after this, there is no substitute for real consulting room experience. Whether you practice on friends, relatives or colleagues matters little but practice you must do!

RAPPORT

The Oxford English dictionary defines rapport as relationship or communication, especially when useful and harmonious! This itself is a perfect description of the first stage of induction. The concept of rapport is not unknown to you. You see it around you all the time, in fact you are already an expert at it, yes you are! Take a look at your friends and family, at people in the street, at parties or in the bars and you will see people in rapport and also people who are quite definitely not in rapport.

A young mother or father with child, lovers looking into each others eyes, old friends comfortable in each others company, two supporters of the same football team recalling the high points of the match, the three people in the corner discussing their mutual concern about political matters and the two drunks who are at each others throats, these are all examples of how you have spotted if people are in rapport (or not) in the past.

Now wait a minute, there is something missing here isn't there? I was talking about and you were thinking about something that we could not possibly have observed, namely thought processes. When we see people together we can't read their minds, can we? We can only observe their bodies and actions and listen to their voices. We don't know if the young lovers are really in love or if they are both secretly having affairs. We couldn't possibly tell if the two old friends are secretly plotting to rob each other or if one of the political discussion group is actually bored to death. What we base our assumptions on are the obvious signs of rapport, the smiles, the laughter, the physical closeness, the relaxed stances, in short its down to body language and voice tone.

Most of our daily communication is non verbal or tonal. That is to say, the way we move our bodies, change our facial expressions and raise or lower our voices communicates more than the actual words themselves do. This is what we have been watching and/or observing all these years and from this we have all become experts at reading peoples minds. I said you are expert at rapport and indeed you are, so much so, you cannot only use your body to mean much more than you say but you can even lie with it.

Imagine this situation. I am willing to bet you have done something similar to this many hundreds of times in the past, perhaps without even noticing it yourself. There is someone you need to impress, a potential employer or the bank manager. Someone from whom you need, but do not like. It may be a situation or an act that you feel is beneath your dignity, asking for a raise or a loan, or maybe trying to convince a policeman that although you shot through a red light you really are a responsible person that can be trusted to never do it again. At times like this your body sings out like an orchestra, your intent and meaning can be read like a neon sign from a dozen yards away, if you watched yourself on a video you would be astonished at just how brilliant you are, and all the time you probably didn't even know you were doing it!

In the hypnotic sense, rapport is exactly the same. Just as unconscious, just as easy and just as natural. Let us examine the mechanics and the purpose of it. The first necessity of rapport is "sameness". I would like to take you back to the two old friends we met earlier. How did you tell they were old friends and not just passing acquaintances? It was their "sameness", they were at "one", they sat facing each other, they spoke in the same tone of voice. If one whispered the other followed suit, if one laughed the other laughed, if one sat with his arms on the table or slouched back and relaxed so would the other. Always they looked into each other's eyes and paid attention. This much you could see but if they were genuinely friendly there would be other things happening that you could not see. Their thought processes would be exactly the same. They would be thinking consciously of the subject under discussion but subconsciously they would be examining each other and every examination of "sameness" would reinforce the belief within their subconscious that they are liked and trusted. Their breathing would become synchronised and their heart beats the same. The tonal qualities of their voices would stay within the same range. They would look into each others eyes at the same time without any obvious signal being given; they are becoming psychologically one, at least as far as is possible.

Before you start to think that I am now going into the realms of hocus-pocus let me assure you that I am not! There was an experiment carried out many years ago, one which would quite rightly be illegal today. Two Oxen were tied together at birth, they were connected at the neck, legs and tail so that they stood, walked and slept for many years side to side and could not move except in unison. When the bonds were removed some years later they naturally enough felt very insecure about this new situation. The bond between them was so strong that they still walked, ate and moved as one for many years after the fastenings were removed. Stopping for food and water at the same time, walking, stopping and turning heads together all as if still tied together. Bonding is as normal and natural in humans as it is in all animals.

The bond between families and friends is as strong as the tethers that those poor Oxen were subjected to, but I hear you cry: how is this of use in the hypnotic induction process? "Sameness" is the key! Get onto the client's own level, don't try and impress or bully. Talk to them in their own style of language, be intellectual with intellectuals and be plain and simple with others. Move as they do, breathe as they do. Observe their body language and respond accordingly. People naturally like and trust people who appear to be the same as them, those who look into their eyes and communicate!

If hypnotism can be summed up in a single small phrase then it is: "The art of communication and the avoidance of conflict!" The greatest sales people in the world are those who have learnt or have naturally the gift of sameness. This is something that you can try for yourself today. Go out and be with someone else whilst being someone else. The signs now that I have alerted you to them are glaringly obvious. One thing to remember though and that is sameness is NOT mimicry. In fact nothing is more likely to get you a punch in the eye than mimicking exactly what a complete stranger does.

Be subtle, listen carefully, and note what he or she does physically out of the corner of your eye and copy it a few seconds later. Only copy what are obviously unintentional body language and not their deliberate actions. If your client is smiling, smile too, but if he is tapping nervously on the table or has a nervous twitch in his eye then leave well alone. Match movement with movement, voice tone with voice tone, language with language, attitude with attitude. But do not attempt to imitate them exactly. Do all of this in a laid back manner and be non-aggressive at all times. Be sympathetic, be caring but never be patronising or condescending. Listen to what they are saying and always remember you have two ears and only one mouth so use them in these proportions. Avoid confrontation and contradiction, agree with what they say or say nothing at all. Praise the praiseworthy thoughts and ideas he or she is imparting and let stupidity and inaccuracy pass over your head unnoticed.

Everyone's natural instinct is to join in conversations, have their voices heard and their opinions too. They also wish to contribute to, or control the situation. But just for once put these quite normal and natural desires to one side, just for the sake of a single experiment. Listen to the other person's view and let that person take the lead. I promise you a very eye opening experience, which is also extremely satisfying, so go on, go and try it! You'll be astounded. For some this technique takes no more than a couple of hours to hone and polish but for others it can take months to undo a lifetime of habit, but it does work for everyone given time and genuine application. Remember it is you that you are trying to change at this stage not others. If you gain nothing else from this course then you will have been given the gift of friendship and ease in the company of others. By the way these are also good methods to use when picking up members of the opposite sex!

In a hypnotic induction the first thing to do is establish rapport. A nice friendly relaxed atmosphere, "sameness" is apparent to you both and you are communicating and feeling on the same level as the client. The client trusts you and is confident to be placed into your hands, if this trust is not established, continue to work on it until it is. When you first start out, no doubt you will try to induce friends and acquaintances. Well YES, it is easier to establish rapport with them but it is also harder to establish trust in your abilities as a hypnotist. After all they know you are new to the subject and that you only bought this course recently. They will say things like "go on then hypnotise me!" and then sit there waiting for you to cast a spell over them. Be prepared for this, be calm, maintain the sameness, explain that it takes some time to hypnotise people and that you are new to the subject (only say this to people who already know the truth) and that you wish to proceed slowly. Make it a bit of a joke, you should both be enjoying yourselves.

A professional, established therapeutic hypnotist does not have these problems of confidence and nor will you when your credentials have been established. Experienced hypnotists obtain rapport instantly and then recognising that the time is right, simply instruct the client to "go into a trance now!" for them and me it's easy (sometimes). The client knows that he is going to be hypnotised, there is no doubt in his mind that he will succumb, so they do, its all down to the power of the moment. Rapport should establish three things as follows: 1) Trust 2) Comfort and 3) Belief. You are then ready to progress to the next stage, which is:

OBSERVATION

By now you will have sharpened your eye as to the body movements of others. Probably for the first time in your life you will really be taking notice of those that talk to you and those you talk to. Observation is an acute version of this. You must be aware of every single movement because these are the tools you will use to induce the first stage of hypnosis. Having established rapport you must now connect even further with the mind of the client. I mentioned earlier that each stage of the hypnotic induction process is lead by the client, this is a case in point. You must show them that you are able to feel what they feel, that you are sharing the same experience with them. In a way this is just sameness but is at a much deeper level. But how can you do this considering you are not a mind reader? Well you don't have to be, you just have to be a body reader. The following is an example of the opening words of a verbal induction. See if you can spot how it's done. It shouldn't be hard for a keen observer like you. Remember these are not magic words that will work for all people in all circumstances but they are typical of a keen and observant hypnotist at work.

"Just sit down and relax, lie back if that's more comfortable. That's right, feel your body being comfortably supported by the couch and the weight of your head sinking down into the cushions. Let the stress in your arms and legs flow effortlessly out as you relax completely and become calm, serene and composed. Take your time there is no rush as you feel relaxation flooding your entire body." Some of the language used here might seem a little strange, the phrasing a little unusual even. But pay no attention to that at present, these are things which I will explain later. What I want you to consider now is the subject matter of what is said. At first it may seem that the subject is relaxation, but look again and bear in mind that we are looking at observation in this section. Go on, go back and read it again.

Can you see all the observations? The client looked uncomfortable sitting up, fell back with a sigh and exhaled deeply when her head touched the cushions, she looked a little hurried and anxious and so had to be reassured, her arms and legs looked stiff and straight with toes pointing straight up and fingers clenched, in short she did not look comfortable in this situation and needed reassurance. The hypnotist (that's you) having obtained rapport, now establishes that they are sharing the same experience! That he has an insight into the client's mind and knows what she is feeling and is a part of it.

If you now take the trouble to go back and read those words again you will see that it truly is the client that is leading and not the hypnotist. By using observations which are feedback to the client as suggestions, as well as rapport, you start to enter the client's mind and are then able to control it.

RECOGNITION

The client will slowly begin to recognise that you are capable of understanding her thoughts. Her arms and hands are stiff for example and you observe this without being told. To her the experience of tense fingers is only a thought, she does not know how obvious it is to the trained observer. She is well aware that you are not reading her mind, after all she is not stupid, but the level of contact between you both is becoming more mental and less verbal. As this link is strengthened you can suggest and control more easily.

LEADERSHIP

You will have noticed in the earlier extract that there are some strange links and connections where different sentences that are not really inter-connected are joined together in a cumbersome way. "Let the stress in your arms and legs flow effortlessly out as you relax completely and become calm, serene and composed." You are aware that the hypnotist's words are only a response to his observations. He has seen a physical tension in the arms and legs and is trying to use it to enter the client's mind. So why not just say "I can tell your legs are tense?" Would this not have the same effect? NO! For one thing it would be far too obvious. The client's mind would be trying to figure out how you did know, and lets face it, it wouldn't be too hard for her to figure out would it? And secondly by giving her a puzzle to sort out you are asking her to think alone and not be guided by you. This "guidance" is "leadership" in the hypnotic sense.

There are two things going on, firstly you are addressing the client's mind and secondly you are leading her in the direction you want, which is relaxation! Relaxation is not necessary or even important in inducing hypnosis, but it is what the client expects and this is helpful. It also relaxes the belief mechanism to obvious benefit. The way in which this works is a little complex and will take a page or two to explain, so please bear with me. You cannot become expert without understanding this method of induction as it is the most basic and commonly used.

Stress is an ancient response, sometimes called the "Fight or Flight" response. When our ancestors were still living in caves there were essentially two types of people…the quick and the dead! When suddenly faced with danger, perhaps whilst partaking of some pleasant and relaxing pastime like sleeping or eating, there had to be an instant and profound reaction. If a wild animal or some member of another tribe attacked them without warning then the entire body would have to be put on a "war footing" those that responded well lived and those slow died! It is not surprising that this particular process of instant and permanent natural selection had a profound effect on the human race.

The mechanics of stress, or the fight or flight response, is to flood the body with adrenaline, increase blood pressure, make immediately available resources of energy, stop any unnecessary functions like digestion, the energy of which at that time can be put to better use elsewhere, fill the muscles with Oxygen and get ready to fight to the death or run like hell! But what has this got to do with you and me today? Well the mechanism still exists and would still work today if called upon to do so. If a mugger or a rapist suddenly confronted you, the threat would create the exact same physical reaction as just detailed.

But just analyse that for a moment, as a mugger is a person who looks much like any other person. They have one head and two eyes, two ears etc. The sight of a person would not normally trigger such a profound effect. Even a shady, wild looking individual if he just passed by you in the street would not produce such a reaction, so what is the trigger? It is your conscious mind that sets things into motion. You see him and compare his actions against the files in your memory banks and he matches one marked "danger" and it is then that things start into motion. Once you see that it is not his actual moves or words that trigger stress but in fact your analysis of and reaction to them, it is far easier to see how more commonplace stress is and how it is triggered. Your mind will push the stress button every time that you are threatened, even if it is only financially, emotionally or in any other way.

The stress function cannot be switched off as easily as it is on. You are prepared to fight but normally do not. While it is true to say that it would ease your stress considerably if you could punch your boss in the eye every time he denied you promotion it is not recommended if you wish to keep your liberty. So the chemicals keep on bubbling around your system causing all kinds of problems, sometimes for day, weeks or months on end, with each stressful event compounding the effect upon your central nervous system.

What has all this to do with hypnosis? During stress your conscious mind is racing, checking everything, analysing all things, checking memory files and sorting out all new information. The entire system is on full alert. If you remember the ancient origins of stress you can then understand why this is so. In a situation where you have to be killed or kill it is your subconscious mind that is checking for every possible opportunity to strike. Checking your opponents every move or action in order to prepare a defense, looking for chances to flee or find a weapon whilst all the time controlling and moving your body in response to this immediate and very real danger. Even under only slight stress it is firing on all cylinders at 110% efficiency. It is, don't forget, this part of the minds operation that you are trying to bypass in order to make direct contact with the subconscious.

In this modern world we are all stressed, to some greater or lesser extent, most of the time therefore you don't have a hope of bypassing the belief system at least that is while the defenses are up and checking every detail. Just as the mind can control the stress reactions of the body, the body can influence the mind. Don't believe me? Let's try a little experiment. Without doing anything special or putting this course down or moving I want you to do one thing for me - SMILE! No don't grin that inane little smirk with no real feeling in it, smile with your whole face, a realistic smile as if you were posing for a photo to be sent to a loved one and keep smiling for a full ten seconds. 1,2,3,4,5,6,7,8,9,10, strange how your mood has lifted isn't it? While you are stressed your body is tense. It remains tense until it is exhausted (and have killed your enemy) the system works like this:

Body still stressed EQUALS enemy still attacking
Enemy still alive EQUALS need more stress
More stress EQUALS more bodily tension
Body still stressed EQUALS enemy still attacking etc!

These are not just ideas of mine, I am trying to explain to you in written terms, the chemical reaction which is going on in your body during stress. It is a cycle that feeds on itself and all the stressful stimuli. The cycle can be broken in your hypnotic client and it has to be broken if you are to make his or her conscious mind and its belief system quieter. Physical relaxation will do this. Look at how the above cycle changes now that I have inserted an element of physical relaxation.

Relaxation EQUALS less stress
Body not stressed EQUALS enemy gone or defeated
No enemy EQUALS no need for stress
Less stress EQUALS less bodily tension
Body relaxed EQUALS mind can now rest

Remember that these are not the client's conscious thoughts but a written description of mass interlinked chemical and nervous reaction in their body. Through physical relaxation comes mental relaxation, a lowering of the defenses of the conscious mind (belief and filing system). A good way to imagine the conscious defenses is to liken them to a guard. Yes that's right a soldier or security guard. Lull it into a false sense of security (relaxation) and then create a subtle diversion (suggestions) before you slip passed without even being noticed.

It sounds like a tall order does it not, controlling a person's innermost defense? That is until you remember that we are all slipping in and out of trances all the time. In your life there must have been times when you couldn't sleep or a friend or loved one has come to you for advice on the same problem and what did you say? Count Sheep! There is hardly a person alive who has not tried this or advised others to do so. This is a bypassing of and a controlling of the conscious mind and a giving up to the subconscious. The image of a sheep is a soft image to most people, that is to say anyone who has not actually seen them up close. We think of them as soft, cuddly and totally unthreatening. They are also completely unexciting. Counting wolves or spiders simply would not do. The job of counting is boring and dull to the extreme. It's so dull it is actually a subconscious activity, you just bring up the file marked counting and the system is fully automatic.

To prove automatic counting, remember that time when you were counting something and your attention was distracted or your mind wandered. You lost count didn't you? We have all had this experience, countless times, this is why we count something that we have to imagine such as sheep and not just numbers. The visualisation of the sheep leaping over a fence is just interesting enough to distract your thoughts away from the exam tomorrow or whatever it is that is keeping you awake. The act of counting has no natural end, like reciting a poem has and so your consciousness is then centred on a soft, pleasant, unthreatening image. The worry/stress is put to one side and you consequently fall asleep at long last. I can hear you all shouting but I've tried counting sheep and it didn't work.

Well it's true to say these techniques are not fool proof and although they work for everyone they do so at different times in their lives. Incidentally if you do have trouble sleeping, due to worries that are so strong that the image of the sheep is not distracting enough, then try counting backwards from 1000, if you get to 500 and are still not asleep then count from there backwards in threes or sevens. If that doesn't work then try subtracting six and three quarters each time. Sooner or later you will find something distracting enough to quieten the problem which is keeping you awake and as such will go to sleep. Bear this in mind and you'll always have a good nights sleep for the rest of your life. The conscious mind can only think of one thing at a time, so make it something that does not trouble you!

Now back to the plot, as with the sheep, the distraction of a swinging watch or flashing light is used to concentrate the mind of the client away from the defensive and then the hypnotist's suggestions seep more easily into the subconscious. Tone of voice is also essential and you'll discover in the next chapter to say certain words with a slightly different tonal quality, more slowly or at a lower pitch so that a new message entirely comes across in an almost subliminal way. Yes it's possible to hide "subliminal" messages within normal spoken sentences even during normal conversation and then the "subliminal" sections will be acted upon. So basically, leadership is the process of taking control of the situation and using what you observe to best advantage by including it within your verbal suggestions.

So you see there are an awful lot of similarities between the process of rapport, observation, recognition and leadership to those of the biofeedback style process of induction as detailed in an earlier chapter. Before ending this chapter it would be worthwhile to point out that 90% of reported illnesses is psychosomatic (caused by the mind) and of the 10% of unreported illnesses almost all of them are psychosomatic. Stress is by far the largest cause of many illnesses both of a psychological and organic nature and to this end the release of stress can be the best cure of all.

Reread this chapter several times and you will without doubt be able to help people with all manners of ills and as such be a most successful therapist. They say that even the common cold is a stress related illness as if you had not been stressed in the first place then your bodily immune system would have been working to full effect and the germs which caused the cold would not have affected you. Even with an organic disease such as Cancer or Aids, stress is by far the client's worst enemy. Stress lowers the immune systems effects and also brings about a negative attitude to the illness in hand.

Remove that stress and give positive thinking suggestions to the client and amazing results often do occur beyond their wildest expectations. How many times do we hear of Cancer/Aids patients who have been given six months to live still being alive, living an OK lifestyle some years later? These documented cases are all proof that positive thinking is a most positive force and when combined with relaxation/stress release can bring about apparently miraculous results.

PART FOUR

PRINCIPLES OF VERBAL PSYCHOLOGY

Suggestions can be both of a positive and negative nature, always aim to make your suggestions positive.

To briefly illustrate how strong a negative suggestion can be, imagine this scenario. A young child climbs onto a wall whilst their mother talks to a friend. The young child starts to run along back and forwards on top of the wall. Suddenly the child's mother turns round and sees her son and shouts out "be careful or you will fall!" The child in turn falls off the wall and gets hurt.

You see in the above example, until told that he could fall, the child did not know it was possible. The mother said "Be careful or **YOU WILL FALL!**" and indeed the negative suggestion of you will fall was then acted upon.

Now this chapter may appear to be very haphazard and of little point. However the point I shall be making and be trying to implant into your mind through the writings of this chapter is that every single word that you say in your role as a hypnotist is of utmost importance. Things, which may appear like casual statements, can and usually do have a strong psychological effect on your clients.

Not only do the words you say have great importance, but even more so the way in which you say them matters also. For example if you said "OK now just close your eyes then sleep and relax" to a client in a raised tone of voice as if shouting, do you really think they would relax? Of course not, however if it was said slowly, in a low tone of voice with each of the words being drawn out then your chances of success would be somewhat better. As a general rule of thumb, sleep/relaxation style suggestions should be given in a slow, deep, monotonous tone of voice with words drawn out and suggesting a downwards (sleepy) motion.

For awakening style suggestions a faster, higher tone of voice with inflection/tone changes would be used and words suggesting an upward (awakening) motion should be used at all times. Monotony and repetition is the trade of the hypnotist. Although, of the two, repetition is by far more important, as whether you sing it, shout it or even whisper it, if it is repeated enough then it will start to have an effect upon the person. So repeat, repeat and repeat some more!

Learn to use your voice. It is a most powerful tool in the consulting room and in everyday life. Listen to people when they speak and you will notice a lot can be learned about their emotions just by the way they are speaking. Are they happy? Sad? Upset? or domineering? Well observe, listen and learn, you will soon uncover the secrets that lie within each person's tone of voice.

When proficient at this with the people that you know well, you'll be able to tell when they are lying or holding something back. In order to help you exercise your voice so that you can use it in a monotone or in a commanding way as you would when giving a client commands, I have included two little exercises below which you must do daily on a regular basis until you become aware how you speak and how to use your voice more effectively.

Firstly here is a poem, which to start with I want you to say with emotion just as the poet would mean it to have been said. When proficient at that, learn to say it in a monotone and then add a commanding overlay to that monotone.

EXAMPLE:

I wandered lonely as a cloud that floats on high or vale and hill. When all at once I saw a crowd, a host of golden daffodil.

WORDSWORTH WROTE IT WITH FEELING

I wandered…………lonely as a cloud……that……floats on high……or vale and hill……….when all at once……I saw a crowd……..a host of golden daffodil!

PAUSE AT THE DOTTED SPACES TO ADD FEELING TO VOICE

The next exercise must be spoken in a monotonous yet commanding manner of speech:

You are tired……..very tired……you want to go to sleep……you cannot keep awake…….you are so tired that you must sleep……….your eyes are tired……you cannot keep them open……you are so tired and sleepy……tired and sleepy…..tired and sleepy……..all you want to do is sleep………sleep……deep……deep sleep!

NOTE:

Repeat that over and over again until you know it off by heart. Master the commanding and decisive tone of voice and you will then be on the way to success as a hypnotist. Remember the craft of any hypnotist on stage or in therapy is suggestion. Yes that's right, repeated suggestion followed by cadence! What's cadence? Simple answer, that old fashioned sleep suggestion is nothing but cadence. Cadence is rhythm and rhythm is powerful.

Remember the story about soldiers marching, who break step to cross over a wooden bridge, so that the cadence of the march will not build up resonance in the structure and cause it to collapse. Just as I mentioned earlier you can tell a lot about a person's emotions and state of mind through their tone of voice.

By now I will have said numerous times that as a hypnotist you must have 100% confidence in yourself and your abilities. Indecision will show both in your body language and your tone of voice. As a hypnotist you must be decisive which means everything will be suggested and spoken in the least number of words possible. You must also appear commanding and confident that any suggestions you give will be enacted upon by the subjects. Remember your subjects are told what to do by suggestions being repeated and also remember:

SUGGESTION CORRECTLY EXPRESSED IS HYPNOSIS

My definition of "correctly" expressed is that it must be spoken in a commanding tone with an air of empathy. You must speak clearly and simplistically as does the majority of the population so that there is no doubt in the client's mind what it is you expect of them. Back to cadence again. Do you know how to chant like the mobs do at football matches? A good piece of poetry is nothing but cadence, cadence is a rhythmic beat… one, two, three, four, up two, three, four etc. Repeat this giving exactly the same intonation to each word and then you have mastered cadence.

Positive and negative suggestions are things which you already use in your everyday life without a second thought. Always be positive where possible in the future! A verbal statement of a negative nature can ruin live's. For example parents often turn their brilliant children into dunces by always telling them that they will never be successful because they are dim and should try harder. How much better it would have been to praise the child on all the good things that it did, the child would be happier, feel better about themselves and go on to achieve far more in life! I repeat, always be positive in all that you say and do.

Your speech must always be clear and decisive, if they are not so, they could be interpreted in a way which could be detrimental to your clients. For example "Would you like to sit in the chair?" This is in fact a question and not a command, what should really have been said is "Sit down in the chair that is directly behind you." This last example is a command and has only one possible interpretation. Make sure all your suggestions are commands with only one interpretation both on stage and in therapy, as you must always give one meaning only commands.

Remember also to use the language that all can always understand. Always be extremely careful what you say when your clients are in trance. A casual word said by you might be taken as a command by your client, which as a direct result, they may then act upon now or in the future. Your voice must at all times be decisive, NEVER ever sound unsure of yourself, never whinge, your voice is your personality on stage and in everyday life or therapy.

I will also say again that to learn anything in life you must keep on repeating it until you get it 100% right. In much the same way you must keep on repeating those sleep suggestions until the subject goes into a trance.

To briefly define hypnotism it is "The art of communication and the avoidance of conflict!" Now I hope you understand just how important your voice really is, as all hypnosis is just a form of effective communication. Tone of voice is essential in all communication. It is possible through the way you speak to hide secret (subliminal) messages in a spoken sentence just by changing the tone of your voice.

Although this may sound a bit like science fiction, allow me to demonstrate. You might say to a client in hypnosis "As you lie there comfortably feeling the weight of your body being supported by the couch you are wondering how it is possible that you will go into a trance." Now obviously this is said in a monotone, you will also be at the same time establishing rapport, observation, recognition and leadership as detailed in the previous chapter. Now if you were to say certain words with a slightly different tonal quality, more slowly or at a lower/higher pitch then another message entirely comes across to the client's subconscious mind and as such is accepted and acted upon without their conscious mind even realising what has happened.

Incidentally this works during normal everyday conversation also, its just a case of making what you actually want the person to do seem like part of an innocent sentence so that when the subliminal voice change technique is used the event occurs and they think its their own idea!

In the following example I have underlined the words which are spoken in a different more commanding pitch/tone of voice. "As you lie there comfortably feeling the weight of your body being supported by the couch you are wondering how it is possible that <u>you will go into a trance.</u>" The subconscious accepts "You will go into a trance" as a direct command but the client does not realise this as they just assume it to be a casual part of the sentence. What is happening here is that the reality mechanisms are being bypassed and the subconscious mind is taking in the information unaided. It isn't as discerning as the conscious and it wasn't designed to be, so the ideas not only go directly in without being checked but are also acted upon without question. If a slightly different tone of voice is used, this is recognised by the subconscious and two separate messages are accepted where normally there would be just one.

To illustrate this "subliminal" technique further, I shall detail the working of a long therapeutic style induction. I have underlined the subliminal (hidden) messages, which are spoken in a slightly different tone of voice so that they are accepted as such. "As you lie there comfortably feeling the weight of your body being supported by the couch you are wondering how it is possible that <u>you will go into a trance now.</u> You don't know if <u>you will go into a trance quickly</u> or if it will take some time. (This includes rapport, observation, recognition and leadership) To really enjoy all these <u>pleasant changes</u> that are occurring in your consciousness. (This is recognition, but done in advance of the clients actually feeling differently which you know they will because they are relaxing) "<u>NOW</u> take a deep breath and hold it, hold it, hold it, hold it, breathe out now and as you do all the tensions in your body will be exhaled along with your hot breath. (Of course their breath is hot, the subject has been holding it in their lungs which are warm for longer than usual! Recognition of this type is very powerful, they will feel the heat and they will relax because of the change in breathing rhythm. They also feel sure you have done this via your hypnotic powers and this reassures them that they WILL succumb to your suggestions.) You are lying here on the couch with your head <u>resting</u> against the soft leather. (The words "lying here" are reassuring. They mean togetherness, you are both experiencing this together, "lying there" means you are apart and is negative) As you close your eyes your heavy eyelids are shutting out the distractions of the world. You are listening only to my voice and are <u>going deeper</u> and <u>deeper</u> within yourself finding that pleasant comfortable place where you can relax totally.

Now start <u>slowly</u> counting <u>backwards in your mind</u> from two hundred, 199, 198, 197, 196, 195, 194 and so on. Here you have offered a gentle distraction for the conscious mind and you have started the counting verbally to reinforce that they must continue counting whilst you deliver suggestions directly to their subconscious mind. Herein lies another important rule of hypnotism, when the conscious mind is distracted and considering something else, any suggestions given to that person will then go directly into the subconscious mind and as such have a deeply profound effect. Whether you use techniques of disorientation and confusion as will be described or something for the client to think of consciously as is the case here, it matters little. Just as long as you keep the conscious mind occupied on something else, whilst suggestions of sleep and relaxation are allowed to go directly into the subconscious.

As all hypnotic inductions are presentation to make the process look impressive, the only true value they really have is to distract the persons conscious mind whilst suggestions are given directly to their subconscious. For example a person is told feet together, hands by your sides, eyes closed, tilt your head well back and concentrate on your deep rhythmic breathing. This is all "dressing", however by concentrating on their breathing they are then distracting the conscious and all suggestions get to the subconscious with ease. This is also why people can be hypnotised so quickly and why to be a good hypnotic subject they must be able to concentrate. If they cannot concentrate you will not be able to distract the conscious mind and will find the induction much harder.

"Keep counting back and back as you feel those muscles around your eyes relax and those beautiful feelings of relaxation and peace spread to your forehead and scalp and to the muscles of your jaw." (You are now in direct touch with their subconscious. The conscious is busy counting, you are not however fully in control yet and the trance state is still very delicate. Any noise or distraction could break the mood. As a person relaxes and stress is removed, certain bodily functions, such as digestion which were running slowly before may start to function again. Tummies rumbling cause the breakdown of trance more than anything else, but if this happens you can handle it like this. "Nothing can disturb us now. There are no secrets between us, no embarrassment or shame, and as you become aware of those comfortable, peaceful feelings of stillness and contentment sinking <u>further down</u> your body, your face relaxes, your expression is now one of serenity, <u>down, down, further down.</u> These (not those) wonderful feelings spread through your neck, shoulders, chest and stomach, right through your arms to your fingertips and through your legs to the ends of your toes." (Check for evidence here that your subject is still counting, lips slightly moving? Rhythmic head or eye movements? (Under the eyelids known as R.E.M's) does he or she seem to be paying more attention to you? Straining to hear your words or to internalise thoughts? If in doubt start the next passage with) "As you continue to count <u>further down</u> I wonder if you have noticed yet that <u>your body is sinking down deeper</u> into the couch. Becoming heavier as it is fully supported in total comfort. Noting the comfort spreading throughout your body as <u>you go deeper</u> your mind is becoming free, free to roam where it will in total comfort and safety. Free of cares or worries, your new awareness is a beautiful place and it is just within your reach. Between you and where you want to be is a tunnel, a tunnel of beautiful lights, a Kaleidoscope of <u>warm</u> sensual <u>colour</u> that you can <u>move through with great ease.</u> Your destination is now only a few paces away, and now you have arrived as you <u>go deeper and deeper to sleep.</u> (Your client will now be in trance and is now where he or she always intended to go, roaming around the subconscious, but you must now act as a guide otherwise the trip will be wasted. It is at this point you would deepen the trance and then proceed with your therapy).

This style of induction is also ideal for psycho-analysis and past life regression, you just need to suggest that the special place they travel to, through the tunnel of lights will be their previous lifetime should they have one and in analysis you suggest that at the end of the tunnel they will have returned to their childhood ages 1 to 7 (the formative years). The subject can then be moved back in time through ages and lifetimes by each time suggesting a journey back through time by way of a tunnel of lights as is done above.

IT IS FRIGHTENING JUST HOW EASY IT IS TO HYPNOTISE PEOPLE WHO VOLUNTEER AND WANT IT TO HAPPEN!

SOME FINAL ADVICE

As a hypnotist you must learn most of what you will say in word-perfect parrot fashion. Although obviously it must not sound like you've done this, to them it's new! In ordinary everyday conversation, one may be forgiven for forgetting the proper words to use, but there is absolutely no excuse for a hypnotist. You are meant to be an expert who knows his/her subject inside out, as such you cannot when giving suggestions with a stammer, stutter or a search around in your mind for the correct words to use. All you say must be precise; it must fully and completely express the suggestion it intends to convey. It must also be constantly recurring so that the expression of it becomes monotonous, for monotony is, as you know by now the great allay of suggestion.

Well that almost concludes this chapter on "verbal psychology" hopefully by now you will have realised that when used correctly your voice is a most powerful tool, which can have a most powerful effect upon people. My final example of how powerful the voice can be is to point out that the style of voice used by a Sergeant Major gets people to obey his every order whereas a doctor's tone of voice reassures you that everything will be OK! So I'll end this chapter by reminding you of one most important thing:

Every effect has a cause and every cause has an effect. See you in the next chapter!

PART FIVE

PRINCIPLES OF PHYSICAL PSYCHOLOGY

What we say verbally is only a minute percentage of what we are always communicating to others. It behoves us as hypnotists to have an understanding of non-verbal communication and body language. So for this chapter I intend to explain the basic points of this subject to you. After reading it, you would be well advised to train yourself to be aware of all your body movements in order to ensure that your non-verbal style of communication matches the message of what you are saying verbally.

Have you ever met someone, taken one look and then decided you want to hit that person? I bet unbeknown to them they were transmitting very negative attitudes through their body language. Remember your physical behaviour is made up from your motives, thoughts, attitudes and feelings of an emotional nature and it is this behaviour that people see. Your behaviour and your appearance combined are the only bits of you that other people can see. It is therefore logical that other people's impressions of you will be based on the behaviour they see, as they have nothing else to analyse you on except this behaviour and your personal appearance.

Your behaviour is like a transmitter, sending out signals to the people who you are dealing with, the signals you send through your body-language are vital because they influence the reactions of the other person and the faith they have in you and your abilities. Remember that behaviour breeds behaviour, also remember that at least 70% of communication is non-verbal and falls within the realms of body language. So it would behove us to at least have a basic understanding of the subject for use in therapy, or even in our everyday lives.

Examples of ways in which non-verbal messages are communicated are as follows:

Vocal pitch and emphasis, speed of speech, breathing, posture, stance, facial expressions, eye contact, eye movements, pupil size, distances and territories, gestures, movements, clothing, dress, status symbols, choice of words and jargon amongst many others.

The most significant features of non-verbal communication are:

Body-language (which is seen/observed)
Voice (Which is heard/listened to)

The body language aspect includes movements, posture, sitting position, use of the arms. Facial expressions, eye-movements, handshake, way of walking, distance from others, style of dress etc.

So remember your success or failure depends on the mastery of body language and the degree to which your words and body language convey the same message that you are trying to transmit. At any given moment your brain can assume an attitude and communicate this to various parts of your body thus promptly responding with specific actions and expressions (body language). The unseen attitude will then have been conveyed to your potential subject without you even speaking and if this is of a negative nature, then you may find that they lose faith in your powers!

A dancer is trained to, at all times, know exactly what their body is doing physically and as a hypnotist, you must train your body in the same way. As a general rule of thumb, your verbal and visual behaviours must compliment each other 100%. Now for some examples of conscious body language signals to set your mind thinking on others:

    1) A raised, clenched fist = A threat.
    2) A raised hand or finger = A request to speak.
    3) A finger to the mouth = Be quiet.
    4) Pointing to the clock = Time to stop.

5) Cupping the hand behind the ear = Speak up please.

Now follow a few examples of unconscious body language signals to set you're mind thinking on the many others which there are:

1) Dilation of the eyes = Interest aroused.
2) Raised shoulders = Tense.
3) Touching the nose = Uncertain.
4) Tilting the head to one side = Interested.
5) Arms and legs crossed = Defensive.
6) Touching of watchstrap = Impatient.

7) Hands behind the head = Feels confident/superior.

By the way, it is the unconscious body language signals which are the most interesting and significant when interpreting other people's moods, attitudes and intentions as often they will say one thing verbally whilst they actually mean another which is shown through their body language. These body signals will always transmit to you the true picture of what they mean. However, do remember when reading body language that you cannot just look at one detail and draw a conclusion from it. In order to get a reasonably good picture of another person's thoughts and feelings from their body language, you should try to assess the body signals as a whole and see them within the context of the present situation as it arises.

Generally speaking, in order to be accurate, at least three signals should be pointing in the same direction. In short, if you observe people a bit and use your common sense it will become quite easy in a short space of time to become a master of body language reading. There are of course many books on this subject which you could buy or better still borrow for free from your local library which will tell you far more than I am able to tell you here.

Confident people such as you must appear such at all times, consequently, you should always look people directly in the eyes and never break eye contact with them. Don't blink your eyes and thrust your chin forward. You should keep your hands and arms away from your face and if standing, should have them down by your sides or together behind you. If standing up, be bold and upright with your back totally straight at all times and if seated, lean back with legs out in front of you. When standing in one place, don't fidget and then you will appear a most confident and relaxed person, in control of both their mind and their body

I'll move next onto the subject of image, that is how you're physical body looks and the state of health you are in. Now you may be thinking what has this got to do with being a hypnotist? In fact it is very relevant indeed, as for example would you visit a smoker to stop smoking? Would you visit a fat person to lose weight? Of course you wouldn't and in just the same way, as a hypnotist, it does little for your credibility to be a smoker, to be overweight or to be dressed in cheap clothing. So stop smoking if you do it, lose some weight if you're a little on the large size and buy the best outfit that money can possibly buy so that you look like a million dollars. The psychology behind this from a client's point of view is that if you are dressed in expensive gear then you must have loads of money and to have lots of money you must be good at your job and so you must be a good hypnotist. And as I've said numerous times now, if they believe in you and your powers then your job will be easy due to belief and expectancy!

A little note on the side, if you're a non-smoking person of an average weight don't be surprised if you are far more successful as a hypnotherapist. Your face and skin are also part of your physical appearance so make sure you treat them well. To sum up in a few words, make sure that from tip to toe, teeth to fingernails and all in between, that all aspects of your physical appearance are clean, smart and tidy and project that successful image which you require.

<u>**PART SIX**</u>

INTRODUCING HYPNOTHERAPY AND PSYCHOTHERAPY

Doctors are good at treating people from the neck downwards. Hypnotists are able to help with any problem that originates from the neck upwards, in other words, from the mind.

Over 90% of all reported illness is psychosomatic, caused by the mind and can be treated successfully with hypnosis, of the 10% that isn't, much of this can be helped with hypnosis.

The principals for therapy are as follows:

1   Get rapport
2   Induce the trance
3   Deepen the trance
4   Ego strengthening/confidence boosting
5   Do the necessary therapy
6   Implant the major post-hypnotic suggestion
7   Awaken them from the trance

You will then be able to earn money from treating people, to stop them smoking, help them lose weight, gain confidence, break habits and all other simple problems. You go to the client's house, or they come to your consulting room. You get rapport by being friendly, taking an interest in their problem and the explaining about hypnosis briefly and what will occur during the session. They are then asked to lie down, or sit in a comfortable chair and commanded to close their eyes. In your early days, until you become more experienced, the moment the subject's eyes are closed, you can remove the scripts from your briefcase and literally just read from the page, the induction, trance deepening, ego strengthening, appropriate therapy, post hypnotic suggestion and then the awakening routine. You here, obviously, replace the scripts into your case just prior to having the patient open their eyes again.

Do not think this may seem like cheating. Your main concern is for the benefit of your client and a successful conclusion to the session. When you have treated a number of people the scripts will have become second nature and you will have no need to refer to your notes. When you feel ready you can then move into the more complex areas of psychological problems and use your psychotherapy skills to address emotional problems and help overcome fears, phobias, panic attacks, etc.

At this point, you can then earn £35 an hour, or more and unlike suggestion therapy, where you see the patient once and they should then be cured, with analysis you are treating deep seated problems of a highly emotional nature. As such, six to twelve sessions approximately are required on average to make the subject come to a solution of the problem of their own accord. Also to abreact, which as you know from a previous chapter means they will then have off loaded the emotion of a past event which has caused them indirectly to be scared of spiders, water or whatever.

As for example, a young child may be sexually abused and this is then "blocked" out of the mind, so not to trouble them. This cause of problems may then manifest itself by, in later life, making the child allergic to rice pudding, milk and other similar foodstuffs, without there being any logical or physical reason for the allergy.

Under analysis, the client may reveal that they were made to have oral sex and as crude as it is, the mind has made a connection between semen and items of a similar consistency and that is why the problems occur. As the old saying goes, "when you find the cause of the problem, remove it and it's gone, then the symptoms will disappear." Here they reveal the cause, their abreaction (emotion) releases (removes) it and the symptom, which in this case is allergy of certain things, disappears as it was just an outwards manifestation of an inwards problem.

Read the chapter which details information about abreactions again, this time viewing it in the context of what I've just said and remembering that if it gets locked into the mind with emotion, then emotion is also needed to unlock it. Then you'll have a better understanding of how psycho-analysis under hypnosis does help people greatly in many ways.

Go to your library and obtain books about Sigmund Freud, Carl Jung and Milton Erickson and read about their theories and you will then have a far greater understanding of how analysis works and helps people to come to a realisation of the underlying cause of their problems. There are subjects such as transference, counter transference and rationalization, which should also be studied.

Psychotherapy can be used without hypnosis. Combined however, the relaxation of hypnosis on the body and mind helps off load information more easily. A clear example of this is that standard psychotherapists take around 100 hours to solve the problem, whereas when hypnosis is used, the problem can usually be solved in no more than twelve one hour sessions.

Another advantage you will find of learning psycho analysis and all about personality types etc. is that you will be able to use this information in your everyday life to assess people. You will instantly be able to tell what type of person the subject is and which style of induction would be best to use upon them, which of course can only be of benefit.

One very true piece of advice, if you expect to treat others problems without yours interfering, then you must first go through sessions of hypno-analysis to release all your skeletons in the closet. Only by doing this will you be a successful therapist and help others. Now you may think you have no need for this, but I know that every person on earth would benefit from six to twelve hours of this treatment and I guarantee it would improve their life in many ways.

ADVANCED HYPNOTHERAPY

Never forget the power which hypnosis possess and always treat your clients with respect. Their senses will be enhanced and sometimes altered but the experience will be very enjoyable, providing you observe the correct guidelines.

One of the main "perception" tools to instill into your client on your first meeting is your expertise and knowledge. If you memorise, or even better use a clipboard containing notes, the following information, you will leave no doubt at all in the mind of your client. Incidentally, if you use a clipboard, you will appear more professional and you will be able to take notes for future reference and if you position your seat so as to conceal the note paper, nothing which is written down will be visible to your client.

THE CONSCIOUS MIND

The conscious mind (around 12% of the total) helps us with daily decision making and thinks out new situations where we have to decide what to do and how to do it. It can hold only a limited number of thoughts and ideas at any one time which is why we often memorise numbers in small chunks of three, for example a nine number (684128472) is much easier to remember as 684 then 128 then472. This is because the conscious mind can hold only between five and nine units of information at any one time.

THE UNCONSCIOUS MIND

The unconscious mind (around 88% of the total) is where we become very interested for the use of hypnosis. This contains all your memories, emotions, imaginations, intelligence and controls the autonomic nervous system which regulates breathing, blood circulation, heart beat etc. All which has ever happened to you and everything you have imagined is stored away in the unconscious mind which acts just like a computer. All the information is stored away and is available to be pulled back at any time.

A good example of this is riding a bike or driving a car. When we are learning to ride or drive, we hit many obstacles. Loosing balance, crunching gears, lack of confidence and Kangaroo petrol! However, as we practice and become familiar with the skills, they automatically become habit and are stored away in the unconscious mind to use at any time in the future. When we become an expert driver or rider, we don't have to think about how to do it, we just do it automatically.

The conscious mind has an automatic resistance to situations. It reasons and rejects certain situations and acts as our defence mechanism and a safety device. Once the defences of the conscious mind have been closed down, the unconscious mind is accessed and instructions and suggestions are acted upon. It is very important to formulate the suggestions in a specific way to ensure they are accepted. The techniques for this will be explained later.

There are still various myths and misconceptions about hypnosis. Some people are still scared at the thought of the experience because they assume they will become unconscious or helpless, but this is not the case. When hypnotised, you are still aware of everything going on around you and you are still seemingly in control, but you are in a heightened state of awareness and have the overwhelming desire to carry out the suggestions given. In the hypnotic trance, you experience a change in awareness. Just as everybody experiences life differently, everybody has a different way of experiencing hypnosis.

Whilst in your consulting room or on a home visit, you must develop a trust partnership with your client. Without this it will be very difficult to obtain the maximum co-operation required for success. A further extension to this is to go through the following checklist with any new client:

1.	Have you been hypnotised at any time in the past?

2.	You will not be harmed by hypnosis.

3.	While hypnotized, you cannot be made to do or say anything against your normal moral principals and beliefs.

4.	No crime has been recorded as being committed as a result of hypnosis.

5.	Ensure the toilet is not required.

6.	Request that your client removes contact lenses, glasses, shoes, releases tight clothing (tie, belt etc.)

7. Emphasize that they do not try too hard. Just listen and follow your instructions.

8. Tell them that they won't feel much different and not to expect anything to happen.

9. Tell them that intelligence, co-operation and concentration always gives the best results.

10. They may be wondering what happens if they don't come round straight away. Tell them it is very unusual for this to happen, although there are ways to deal with it (see earlier) and if it does happen, it is most likely because they are enjoying the sensations so much that they want to prolong it.

11. A lot of people are a little apprehensive before they are hypnotised for the first time, but afterwards, they experience it as being a pleasant, relaxing state leaving them feeling wonderful.

12. They may be surprised to learn that while hypnotised, they will still be aware and still be able to hear everything around them, it just won't bother them.

13. Ask them. "How do you expect me to hypnotise you?"

The answer to the last question has two reasons. Firstly you will establish the depth of trance estimated. (Deeper and quicker if they have been hypnotised before). Secondly, you are introducing the expectancy and acceptance that you **are** going to hypnotise them.

<u>IMPORTANT MIND RULES</u>

Mindrule One: EACH IDEA OR THOUGHT GIVES A PHYSICAL REACTION

As you will soon come to realise, your thoughts can affect all the functions of your body. Fear, stress, worry and anxiety can all lead to bodily changes

Thoughts with strong emotions almost always reach the unconscious mind and once accepted, these thoughts carry on producing the physical reactions. To reverse this effect, the unconscious mind must be accessed to change the thought pattern.

Mindrule Two: EXPECTANCY IS REALISED

Our brain and nervous system respond to thoughts and images. Our physical health is largely dependant on our mental expectancy. Doctors recognise that if the patient expects to recover quickly, then they are more likely to. On the other hand if they expect their condition to worsen, then it often does. Negative attitudes bring negative results. Positive attitudes bring positive results.

Mindrule Three: SYMPTOMS, INDUCED EMOTIONALLY FOR LONG ENOUGH CAN CAUSE ORGANIC CHANGE

It is believed that in excess of 70% of human ailments are functional rather than organic, i.e. the organs of the body are affected by the reaction of the nervous system through negative ideas in the mind. This is not to suggest that everyone with an ailment is neurotic, there is disease causing illness, but if you continue to complain, fear and think about your nervous headaches or tensed up stomach, then organic changes will occur in time.

Mindrule Four: IMAGINATION IS MORE POWERFUL THAN KNOWLEDGE IN THE MIND

This is especially important when using self hypnosis. We often feel superior to people who have been tricked in some way, but we are also blind to the facts of our own unreasonable beliefs. A thought or idea supported by a strong emotion such as anger or hate is often difficult to alter through normal reasoning but easily addressed through hypnosis.

Mindrule Five: AN IDEA REMAINS, UNTIL IT IS REPLACED BY ANOTHER, IN THE UNCONSCIOUS MIND

If an idea is accepted in the unconscious mind, it stays there. The longer it remains, the more it becomes habit and part of our normal daily lives, whether it is good or bad.

To change our actions, we must first change our thoughts. We accept known facts such as 2+2=4 and the sun and moon are up there even though we cannot see them. But we often get programmed into thinking, " I must have a cigarette with my coffee" or "I must eat my lunch at 12.30." These are not actually correct, but have developed into a fixed habit and there will be a conscious resistance to changing them. Changing them unconsciously however, will bring about permanent results.

Mindrule Six: AT THE SAME TIME, OPPOSING IDEAS CANNOT BE HELD

This is not to say that more than one idea cannot be remembered, but means that there will always be a conscious conflict to opposing ideas. If you try to preach one thing while actually practicing another, then the nervous system will have a negative response to the conflict.

Mindrule Seven: THE MORE CONSCIOUS EFFORT, THE LESS SUBCONSCIOUS RESPONSE

When dealing with the subconscious mind, do not rush. Work in a methodical manner to develop positive mental expectancy. Do not force anything, just let things happen naturally. The more you "try" the less effective the results will be. Encourage your client to just listen, relax, co-operate etc.

PRE CONDITIONING

If you are happy that your client is willing to commence quickly you can start the induction, but if there is apprehension or you suspect they do not believe they will be hypnotised, the following usually provides adequate proof for therapy.

Take a ring, small weight or key and tie a length of string to it about eight inches long and tie the other end to the end of a pencil. Next, take a sheet of A4 paper and draw a bold straight line on it about six inches long down the middle. Place the paper on your desk or table and tell your client to stand in front of the paper, hold the pencil between the end of their thumb and forefinger, with the ring about one inch above the line, in effect making a miniature fishing rod. Ensure the elbows are not touching the body and start to give instructions as follows:

"As you stand concentrating on the line at all times, allow your mind to focus only on this. Just gaze at the line. Don't think about anything else apart from the line. As you gaze and concentrate, you will soon find that the weight will start to swing backwards and forwards, along the length of the line. Concentrate all your attentions on the line and as you do, you will find the weight will start to swing up and down along the length. The harder you concentrate, the more the weight will swing. Allow your mind to think only of the weight starting to swing up and down the length of the line."

Keep repeating these suggestions and vary them slightly if you wish until the weight starts to swing. Your client will be amazed by the apparent power you are demonstrating. (Try this experiment on yourself by using the focus of your imagination to get the weight swinging).

While the weight is swinging, you can then start suggesting that if an ellipse or circle is imagined, the weight will follow these shapes. Just keep repeating in a confident manner until it happens.

It is important that you encourage a positive response from your client because if thoughts such as "I don't think it will work for me" or "It is not moving" will probably result in the weight staying put as both the conscious and unconscious mind will have accepted negative thoughts. With success in this, you will have surprised your client how quickly you can exert your "power" and they will be ready to co-operate for hypnosis.

An alternative to this could be to lock your clients eyes closed within a matter of seconds. This method has been explained in the Stage Hypnosis course, but a suitable routine and narration for the consulting room would be as follows:

Ask your client to sit comfortably in a chair and stand in front and slightly to the side of them. Explain in a confident manner that you are now going to demonstrate how you are going to simply and quickly lock their eyes closed so that they will not be able to open them until you say so. Take a pencil and starting around six inches centrally in front of their face, instruct them to follow the pencil wherever it goes without moving their head. Now move the pencil slowly from side to side, gradually increasing the distance you move it. Tell them to try and watch the pencil, even when it goes out of sight. After moving from side to side four or five times, alter the movement to up and down and again, gradually increase the distance you move the pencil. Tell them to try and follow it, even when it goes out of sight above or below the field of vision. This will have a slightly disorientating effect and lead you on to the next stage.

When you have completed this routine, tell your client to close their eyes normally and let them relax for a few moments. Then with your finger, touch the point on their forehead which is mid way between the eyebrows and half way up the forehead i.e. the exact point where you would imagine the third eye to be. Instruct your client to leave their eyelids closed and at the same time, try to look at the point on their forehead which you are touching (you should be able to see the eyes under the eyelids move upwards). Now, with an authoritative tone, instruct them to continue to try and look at the point on the forehead and focus their attention there. Repeat these suggestions and ensure their eyes are still in that position (don't leave this too long as it may become uncomfortable) and then say in a confident and positive manner. "Now you can not open your eyes! You can **not** open your eyes. Continue to look at the spot and however hard you try, you can not open your eyes. The harder you try to open your eyes, the tighter they will stick together. You will not be able to open your eyes until I tell you that you can."

This method, if used correctly, will work every time because of the muscle arrangements around the eyes. At this point you can either tell them to relax and stop concentrating on the spot and then they will be able to open their eyes, or leave them in this state and start the induction directly from here. (You should of course tell them to relax their eyes, stop looking at the spot and let them remain closed)

There are many favourable conditions for your consulting room which will prove beneficial. First and foremost, a reclining chair or couch should be used. When preparing for your induction, it is best to ask your client for their preference on how they feel most comfortable. You may be surprised that some (especially female, if you are male) feel a little vulnerable if reclined fully back in a chair. The best advice is to let them decide, and then there will be a minimum of resistance from them.

Ensure the room is warm and as quiet as possible and avoid any bright lights shining directly on your clients face. Some people prefer to work in a dimmed room with a light bulb of 15 to 20 watts, but this is down to personal preference. What is a major asset however to therapy is blue light. For the consulting room, both the décor and the lighting have positive influential effects when used around the theme of blue. It is perfectly adequate to obtain a number of blue light bulbs from your local DIY store and replace the existing ones, - bear in mind however that even a 60 watt blue bulb will provide very little actual light and you may need a number of them in a larger room – if you are using a spare room in the house, you may prefer to set up your own "hypnotising light arrangement" on a portable stand with two or three bulbs arranged on it. This can then be placed to the side of your client as and when required.

Soft relaxing music in the background will help with the induction routine. A shadow tape (see web site for details on shadow tape) will work well, even better if you record one of your own with your own voice. If you prefer however, audio cassettes and CD's are available from libraries and High Street shops. A little forward planning is required here though, as the length of the tracks may only be four or five minutes and you will need (especially in the early stages) possibly twenty to thirty minutes of continuous music. It is much better to copy a number of suitable tracks onto a CD or tape without breaks (watch out for copyright laws) and use this for your induction sessions. You can vary your choice of music and build up a selection to use with different types of clients, but always ensure the music is of a soft and relaxing nature and play it at a lower volume than the level of your voice.

Your preparation aim is to influence as many of the senses as possible. You have now addressed the sense of sight (blue light), touch (warm room and limited movement) and hearing (soft music). There is little you can do about the sense of taste at this stage but the sense of smell can have an immense influence.

The art of Aromatherapy is based on the sense of smell, influencing the Olfactory Nervous System which now proves so successful that the therapy is being introduced into intensive care units of hospitals. The natural oils have different effects on the frame of mind and can be stimulating, sedative, rejuvenating, warming, refreshing or relaxing. For this reason, a blend of Lavender and Frankincense in a small oil burner within the room will be invaluable. Lavender is well known for its relaxing and sedative properties while Frankincense encourages deeper breathing.

To repeat again, as it is vitally important for therapy also, the manner in which you speak is very important. Use a quite but firm tone of voice which leaves no doubt at all in your client's mind that you are fully confident and know what you are doing. While making your suggestions, there should be a minimum of pauses and your delivery should flow smoothly. Postcard sized cards can be used to refer to. Don't worry about your client seeing the cards as they will have their eyes closed, simply conceal them from view until they are no longer open.

Before you start, ask if the toilet is required, make sure a comfortable seating or lying arrangement has been taken and release any tight or restrictive clothing (untie or remove shoes, slacken belt, loosen any clothing around the neck etc.)

PART SEVEN

INDUCTION METHODS FOR THE CONSULTING ROOM

The simplest things are usually the most effective in life and hypnosis is no exception. The process of hypnosis is so easy to carry out, that, for most, it's hard to believe it works and yet, that's exactly the reason why it's so effective, as people believe you must be doing something complicated to place them into trance. But you should have learnt the true secret off by heart now and that's the fact it's all down to belief and expectancy and following the simple steps, which I am explaining to you in this course, then success will be yours.

By now, you will have hopefully assimilated all the other knowledge which I have revealed to you, if not, then please go back to page one, read through it all again and digest until you do understand what I've said. As you must understand what I've said in order to understand how these hypnotic inductions actually do work. The fact is that people are already 90% on the way to already being hypnotised before they step into your consulting room, due to your advertising etc. If you have followed all these points mentioned so far in this course, and the client in your consulting room believes you are a professional hypnotist, with the skill to place them into trance and they also expect whatever you do to work, then as hard as it is to believe at this moment in time, it will work.

So follow the guidelines and you'll have great success with your hypnotic inductions. Practice, practice and practice some more. Remember this though, don't try it out on family and friends and expect a huge success, as they knew you when you weren't a hypnotist, so that most vital element of belief and expectancy will not be there.

THE PROGRESSIVE RELAXATION INDUCTION

This induction, as the title suggests, is slow and progressive. For these styles of inductions the client must be sitting on their chair or lying on a couch or bed. You will find that the wording for such an induction (with added subliminal effects) is in the verbal psychology chapter of this book, and basically, it just relies upon the principles of rapport, observation, recognition and leadership, which are also described in full elsewhere.

What you say to the subject/s will be different each time and dictated by the way in which the subject/s react to you suggestions. (Always use what the majority do as your guide.) Of course the standard phrases, which all hypnotists use at some time, and are included at the end of this chapter, will come in extremely useful during a progressive relaxation induction. Follow all that you've been taught, and the example induction as given in the earlier chapter and you will be able to carry out a progressive relaxation induction. As you will by now know, the basic techniques of what makes an induction work and of how rapport, observation, recognition and leadership dictate what you say to the subjects in a progressive relaxation induction, I will now give a few examples of additional distractions which can be offered to the subjects mind to promote the onset of trance more rapidly.

THE SIDNEY FLOWERS BLINK METHOD OF P.R.I.

This is in essence a progressive relaxation induction (P.R.I), which is also combined with a method to strain the client's eyes. The client is seated as for other P.R.I.'s and is told to focus upon a spotlight, or a point on the ceiling, which they are not to take their eyes off (this also helps strain the eyes). You then explain that you will be counting, and on each number everyone will get more and more relaxed, and within a few short moments, everyone will find it so much easier to let their eyelids, which will become so heavy and tired, to shut, rather than trying to keep them open. You also explain that on each odd number as you count, they should close their eyes and on each even number, they should re open their eyes. For example:

On 1…….. eyes shut

On 2…….. eyes open
On 3…….. eyes shut
On 4…….. eyes open
On 5…….. eyes shut
On 6…….. eyes open
On 7…….. eyes shut (etc)

So that on each alternate number, from one they have to shut their eyes and then re-open them on the next even number count. Combine this with the fact they are staring at one point all the time and I'm sure, you can understand why their eyes become strained so quickly. And as the littler muscles in the corner of the eyes do become tired, they will find it much easier to allow their eyes to remain shut. You use your normal patter, which is formulated at the time through a combination of the standard phrases and the things that come to mind, due to rapport, observation, recognition and leadership. Obviously you will also keep suggesting that their eyes are becoming so tired and that their eyelids are becoming so heavy, so tired, so limp, loose and relaxed, as each second passes by. By the count of thirty, most, if not all people, will have had their eyes closed for a while already, however, if their should still be the odd one or two with eyes open, this is now the time to command everyone to close their eyes, and you then proceed directly into your trance deepening patter, to take them all to a deeper level of trance, in a very short space of time.

SPOTLIGHT EYESTRAIN P.R.I.

To cut a long story short, the principles used are identical to any other P.R.I., except, that here, it is very bright spotlights that strain their eyes and disorientate them, as you deliver your suggestions of relaxation as usual. For the consulting room, it can simply be a spotlight mounted on a wall. The lights should be above the client's normal eye level, so that they must strain their eyes in the first place in order to see the light. Add to this the intensity of the bright white spotlight itself and maybe now you can see why they become lethargic, their eyes glaze and then close and they do exactly as you say.

MUSCULAR RELAXATION P.R.I.

Very briefly, the principles are the same except here, they start with their eyes closed and you suggest that, as you mention different areas of their body, they are to imagine the muscles in that area of their body as ropes tied together in knots, and as they mentally undo the knots in their mind so that they become separate lengths of rope, so, in reality, all the muscles in that bodily area, will become so limp, so loose and so relaxed, as they also become so heavy and so tired. You start with their feet, and move around their body, getting them to imagine the same thing happening for their ankles, lower leg area, knees, upper leg area, hips and thighs, groin area, stomach, chest, back, spine, shoulders, shoulder blades, the whole arm area, wrist, hands, fingertips, neck, jaw, cheeks, brow muscles etc.

Each time getting them to visualise the relaxation and each time telling them that as the knots untie and the ropes become separate, so in reality all the muscles in that area, will instantly become so limp, so loose, so relaxed, so heavy and so tired, with each and every breath that they take. You also, at various intervals along the way, insert some of the standard phrases, such as "The deeper you go, the better you feel and the better you feel, the deeper you will go." By the time you've gone round their entire body in this vein and have reached their heads, you will find that they are in a deep trance, and at this point, you would immediately deepen the trance further in the standard way. At the end, you would then say "Sleep" firmly and implant your post-hypnotic suggestions. This induction when done nice and slowly, which is why it's called a P.R.I., should take between six to ten minutes, dependent upon your speed of delivery.

THE COUNTING BACKWARDS INDUCTION

This induction is exactly as the name suggests. (Refer to the verbal psychology section for an example of this type of induction). The client is asked to keep counting backwards in their mind. You keep setting the pace of counting in their mind until you've gone back to 180 and then it's left to them to continue doing so in their minds, which distracts their conscious mind. Therefore all suggestions given go directly into the subconscious mind. Your pace of wording should be such that it suggests relaxation and then you end the induction as per the example in verbal psychology chapter. This whole induction should last no more than five minutes in total, from start to finish.

The four methods which follow are ideal for the consulting room and will take most clients into a light state of trance where little or no reaction to suggestion will be obtained. To obtain maximum response, it is necessary to deepen the state and this is covered a little later.

FIXED GAZE INDUCTION

With your client seated comfortably take a pencil or something similar with a shiny end. Instruct your client to take a number or deep breaths and on inhaling totally, hold the breath for a few moments, then release slowly and fully. Repeat this three or four times. Hold the shiny end of the pencil slightly higher than the level of the gaze and about ten inches away from the face and ask your client to gaze and concentrate constantly at the end of the pencil. As the elevated position of the eyes is maintained for a period, the muscles will tire. This is because the eyes are pulled inwards and upwards and are not accustomed to the strained position. The tiring of the eyes is a psychological process and you should anticipate, by observing, when the eye muscles are becoming tired. When this appears to be starting to happen you start your suggestions by saying something similar to: "Your eyes will soon begin to feel heavy. Your eyes will feel tired. Your eyelids will feel heavy and tired. Your eyes are now felling more and more tired. Your eyelids will feel so heavy, they will want to close. You are getting sleepier as you gaze at the pencil. Your eyes are now feeling so heavy, they will want to close down". If you observe any blinking of the eyelids say "You will find your eyelids starting to blink and as they do, your eyes will feel even more heavy and tired."

Keep repeating suggestions of heaviness, sleepiness, tiredness of the eyes etc. until your client's eyes close down. When the eyes are closed **YOU HAVE HYPNOTISED YOUR CLIENT!** You have closed their eyes with the power of suggestion. Simple as that. This maybe true, but you have only guided your client into a light hypnotic trance at this stage. You must now go through the process of deepening the state to ensure the post hypnotic suggestions are as effective as possible.

A number of other techniques now follow and to avoid repetition, as with the above method, the explanation will be only to this light stage, as fuller and more detailed instructions for deepening the state are given later and are common to each light trance induction.

VISUALISATION METHOD

Assuming your subject is comfortably seated and has gone through the deep breathing routine; say something similar to "Now just close your eyes. That's right, allow your eyes to close down and let yourself relax, let yourself feel comfortable, let all the tensions in your body start to fade away. Now with your eyes closed at all times, I want you to visualise the letter O or zero in your mind. See the circle in your imagination and now put it on a flat piece of wood in front of you. Now take an imaginary pen and draw another circle, a little smaller this time on top of the first one so you now have the figure of 8. You will now see the figure of 8 which is the small circle on top of the large circle. Now, take your pen again and fill in the centres of the two circles so now have two circular discs or wheels. Take the small one off the top of the large one and place it carefully on the piece of wood at the side it. Now take a small paint brush with the bristles loaded with white paint and draw a spiral on each circular disc so both look like the end of a swiss roll. Now, tilt the piece of wood slightly to your right and watch them swirl along the piece of wood right to the end, the piece of wood can be as long as you like, watch them swirling away to your right. When they reach the end of the wood they will stop. Now tilt the shelf to your left and watch them swirling off to your left. See them as they come whirling and spinning to your left. From your left now, with the wood tilted slightly to your right, watch them come spinning back. Just to the centre from where they started and…… stop. Now take a rubber and rub out the middle of the discs so you are left with the two original circles and place the small one on top of the large one and you will have the figure of 8 back. Now let the small circle on top start to disintegrate into dust and disappear. Totally disappear. You are now left with nothing at all so just let yourself relax and let your mind go blank. As all the images and pictures disappear let all the sounds fade away into the distance. Just relax, let your body start to feel heavy. Feeling sleepy. Sleep deeply. Pay no attention at all to any sounds, apart from the sound of my voice. All the other sounds fade away into the distance. Feeling drowsy and sleepier. Just listening to the sound of my voice. You're sinking further and further down. With every breath you take you're drifting down dee-per and dee-per. All of your muscles releasing and letting go completely. Your mind and body letting go completely, everything letting go and feeling very relaxed --- heavy --- comfortable. Nothing at all will disturb you sinking down still deeper. [Commence deepening routines].

FOCUS OF CONCENTRATION METHOD

Assuming your subject is comfortably seated and has gone through the deep breathing routine say; "For the next few moments just let your arms rest comfortably on the chair arms or on your thighs. Let them relax and go limp. Let them feel heavy. Let all the muscles in your arms relax. In a moment I will place my hand in front of your face and I want you to concentrate on my middle finger." Place your hand in front of your client's face with your middle finger above the line of vision and about eight inches away. Hold this position for a few moments then continue "In a few moments I will bring my hand down in front of your face and when I do, just follow my middle finger downwards which will cause your eyes to close. Follow my finger downwards and close your eyes. Now, keep your eyes focused on my middle finger and follow it down as it passes in front of your face and let your eyelids close down." Pass your hand slowly down in front of your client's face until their eyes close down then continue "Now your eyes are comfortably closed down, let all the little muscles around them relax. Let all the tiny muscles around your eyes let go. Let them feel heavy and even more relaxed. Let them release all the tensions to such a point as they would not work at all even if you wanted them to. When you have let them relax to such a point and not before, that they would not work even if you wanted them to, test them. When you have let them relax so much that they will not work, you have been completely successful. Re---lax. Re—l—ax. Well done, now stop trying and let the whole of your body relax in the same way. Your whole body relaxing and feeling heavier. I will now take your hand and lift your arm slightly into the air. As I lift it, let the muscles release and let go even more, so your hand and arm hang loose and limp. Then when I let go, let it fall like a heavy weight of lead. When your hand touches your body I want you to send a surging wave of relaxation right from the top of your head all the way down to the very tips of your toes. This will double your level of relaxation and make you feel twice as comfortable". Take the hand and continue "I'm raising your hand now. Just let it hang loose. Let it feel heavy and limp. Let all the muscles let go. That's right, that's fine. Now when I drop it, let it fall like a heavy weight of lead to your body. When it touches your body feel the surging wave of relaxation move from the top of your head to the tips of your toes". Let the hand go and direct it to fall onto the upper legs and when it touches emphasize the relaxation by saying "Waves of relaxation sweeping through your body" or something similar. Then repeat the process with your clients other hand. [Continue with deepening routines].

THE COUNTING METHOD

Assuming your client is comfortably seated and has gone through the deep breathing routine. Arrange a low wattage blue light bulb or a blue disc which you can illuminate in a position which is easy for your client to gaze at. Ensure the rest of the room is in subdued light. Now tell your subject to fix all attentions and concentrations on the light or illuminated disc and follow your instructions. Then say that when you count "one" they should close their eyes and when you say "two" they should open them, when you count "three" they will close them and when you count "four" they will open them. Tell your client that you will continue to count and with every odd number they will close their eyes and with every even number they will open them. Then say "As I continue to count, you will find that your eyelids start to feel drowsy, your eyes will become heavier and heavier with every number. As I count further you will experience an increasing resistance to open your eyes which will grow stronger with every number. Your eyes will soon become so heavy and tired and the resistance to open them will be such that you will not be able to open them any more. When you find you are unable to open them, do not worry, just let them stay comfortably closed and relax and continue listening to me."

It is not necessary to indicate how long this will take, but you could say for example, that by the time you reach twenty the eyelids will feeling heavy. This will be down to your judgement based on your previous tests. As you start to count, make the pause after the odd numbers be progressively longer than the pause after the even numbers. Do not make this too obvious at first, but lead into it gradually. The result of this is that your client's eyes are closed for a longer period than they are open. Keep a smooth rhythm which will avoid any tenseness or uncertainty which you must avoid. As you reach the number twenty, observe what is happening. If it appears your client's eyes are starting to close voluntarily then continue counting. If there appears to be resistance, then amplify the suggestions by saying something like, "20 -- 21 you are feeling very relaxed. 22 -- 23 you are resting very comfortably in the chair. 24 -- 25 your eyes are becoming heavier and heavier. 26 -- 27 you are resting pleasantly and quietly. 28 -- 29 your eyelids are becoming heavier and heavier. 30 -- 31 it is now becoming too much of an effort to keep your eyes open. 32 -- 33 they are getting so heavy and tired, it's too much of an effort and your eyes want to stay closed. 34 -- 35 it's much more pleasant to sit resting with your eyes closed as they are so heavy. 36 -- 37 your eyes are so heavy and all you want to do is rest quietly and peacefully."

Make sure that you comment on the odd numbers while the eyes are closed and when they stay closed continue with the deepening routine given below.

DEEPENING THE HYPNOTIC TRANCE

You should now be proficient at inducing a light trance in your client which is a state little different to the normal waking state. To ensure your suggestions have maximum results, you must go through a number of procedures to deepen the hypnotic trance progressively. Each routine takes your client deeper every time and influences the next one. It is only a matter of guiding by talking patiently and observing the responses. When you get a little further through the routines, you will be able to awaken your client and return them into a deeper trance by simply saying the word "sleep."

A number of observations should be noted as you go through your deepening routines as these will provide you with a guide. It is always difficult to gauge the actual depth of hypnosis but as you become more experienced you will notice these reactions and be able to assess the depth.

- The face often changes in appearance and turns to a slightly wax like shade.
- Reflex actions start, such as: swallowing, twitching fingers, breathing deepens.
- Spasmodic movements start, such as: frowns, rolling of the eyes under the eyelids.
- The head often falls to one side or forwards.
- The lower jaw often falls open a little.
- There is an appearance of total muscle relaxation in the whole body.
- There is an apparent total reluctance to move.

Remember the senses mentioned earlier (sight, hearing, touch, smell and taste) as these are very important now. The more senses you are able to bring into the induction, the more effective it will be. An excellent example would be: "As you lie on the soft golden sand you can feel the warm summer sun beating down on your body. You may be able to hear the birds singing in the distance and smell the sweet scents of the flowers drifting over the cliffs. You can see the leaves of the palm trees gently rustling in the warm breeze and hear the sound of the sea, gently lapping up the coastline". Sentences such as these are very expressive and use descriptive words to make it easy for your client to visualise. This is exactly what you want.

Below is an example of what to say to start the deepening procedure. It has been purposely kept quite long to give you a good idea of the style and repetitiveness required. You can either use a copy of this or devise your own, but always remember to use a monotonous tone. As you become more experienced you will find that a shortened version of this will only be required. This speech should be started when your client has closed their eyes and spoken in a slow, methodical manner and you could start your music at this point for extra effect. Emphasize the words in italics, but not too obviously. The aim is to guide your subject into a deep state of physical and mental relaxation which will then close down the conscious mind and allow you direct access to the unconscious.

It is assumed your client is sitting in a chair. If however, they are lying down, amend your suggestions to suit.

"As you sit peacefully in the chair (or lie on the bed or couch) I want you to remain *comfortable* and allow your eyes to remain closed and just listen to my voice. Just *let go* of all the tensions and *enjoy* the feeling of being relaxed. *Now,* as you sit comfortably relaxed, let all your thoughts drift away. Don't think about anything apart from what I am saying and think only of that. *Now,* I want you to think for a few moments and think about --------- (slight pause) *weightlessness.* Just think about *weightlessness.* What it must feel like to be weightless. You may have thought about it before or seen it on a film. Think about becoming weightless. Your whole body feeling lighter than air and *relaxing* even more. Weightlessness. It's just as if you're floating away on a cushion of air which moulds itself perfectly to all the contours of your body and supports it. Feeling lighter than air and *weightless.* Now beginning to float and drift away to anywhere you like. And you can now start to relax your whole body even more, drifting *deeper* into comfortable relaxation and continuing just to rest peacefully. Your whole body continuing to relax even more, starting with your feet. Just imagine for a moment, imagine in your minds eye, imagine your toes and all the little muscles round them. See them in your mind and *feel* them relaxing. Let them go limp. Let them go heavy. Feel all the tensions just fading away. Limp and heavy. Now your feet, both feet. Feel them relaxing. Going heavy, feeling just like lead. Both feet, totally relaxing, getting *heavier* and *heavier.* Now starting to move up your legs, moving up both legs, all the way up to your knees. *Relaxing.* Your calf muscles, *relaxing,* feeling heavy, all the tensions just fading away. Now moving further up your legs, up both legs, to you thighs, *relaxing,* feeling *heavy.* Now just ask yourself if there is any tension at all left in your feet and legs ----------- and if there is, let it *smooth* away. Calmly let it smooth away and your legs will become even heavier. Now slowly moving further up you body, through your stomach, right up through your chest, *relaxing,* all the way up to your neck, *relaxing.* Your stomach, your chest, all the way up to your neck, *relaxing.* Feeling *heavier* and *heavier.* All the tensions, *completely* fading away. All the muscles letting go completely. Now you back, your whole back, right from your thighs to your neck, all the muscles in your back, *relaxing,* feeling heavy. As your back relaxes even more, enjoy the feelings and now let your shoulders *relax,* your shoulders relaxing and feeling heavy. All the muscles in your back and your shoulders, *relaxing,* going limp and *heavy.* Now your arms, moving down both arms, to your elbows, *relaxing,* further down your arms, right into your hands and flowing through your fingers and thumbs, *relaxing,* feeling heavier and heavier. With every breath you take and with every word you hear, you are sinking *down* further and further into deep relaxation. Your shoulders now relaxing even more and starting to droop as they feel even *heavier.* Your whole body feeling heavy and relaxed, with no effort at all. Now, as you rest feeling wonderfully calm and peaceful, just think for a few moments about your breathing. Allow your thoughts to dwell on your breathing, because when we're asleep we don't have to think about our breathing, our body does it for us. So do that now, think about your breathing and be aware of your breathing, but just let it happen naturally. Focus upon it and be aware of your body taking in just the right amount of air. As you breathe out, you are breathing out tension and as you breathe in you are becoming more and more relaxed. Every time you breathe in, you are becoming more and more relaxed and every time you breath out you are releasing more and more tension from your body. You don't need to make any effort at all, just let it happen and let it happen naturally. Your whole body now relaxed and now moving up you neck. Moving up your neck and the back of your head, *relaxing.* Up the back of your head and over the top of your head. *Relaxing,* feeling *heavy.* Now down over your forehead, all the little muscles in your forehead, *relaxing.* Now round your eyes. All the tiny little muscles round your eyes and your eyelids, *relaxing,* feeling heavier and *heavier.* Even your nose, your ears, your cheeks, relaxing. Your lips and your jaw, feeling heavy. Even your tongue inside your mouth, *relaxing.* You will find, with every breath you take, you are drifting down deeper and *deeper* and getting sleepier and sleepier. Now as I count from ten to one, you will find yourself drifting down even deeper to sleep and feel even heavier. *Ten,* relaxing more with every number I count. *Nine,* feeling heavier. *Eight,* heavier and heavier with every number. *Seven,* getting sleepier. *Six,* drifting deeper to sleep with every number. *Five,* feeling yourself being dragged down even deeper. *Four,* sleepier and sleepier. *Three,* heavier and heavier. *Two,* almost there, feeling so heavy and sleepy and *One,* so deeply relaxed now feeling wonderfully calm, peaceful and tranquil. Sleeping deeply where nothing at all will disturb you".

At this stage, your client should be in a deeper state of hypnosis and will probably respond to further suggestions but you should continue with the deepening routine and include visualisation techniques explained below until you become a little more experienced. Remember, your client is still aware of everything which is being said and done so don't rush anything:

"You're sitting comfortably in the chair doing nothing at all but resting. You can hear my voice speaking to you all the time, but it won't disturb you at all. Nothing at all will disturb you. You will find, as you sit there, that your mind is becoming sleepier and sleepier. You won't try to think about what I'm saying, but you will hear everything. As I talk, you will find that your heavy, limp body will start to relax even more and with every breath you take you will find yourself sinking further and further d-o-w-n deeper and deeper getting sleepier and sleepier with every breath. One part of your mind is now already asleep, but you will continue to hear everything I say. Your mind is now at quiet peacefully rest. You will soon find the whole of your body will start to have sensations of tingling.

Pleasant tingling sensations throughout your entire body. Tingling, more and more feeling good. It won't disturb you at all and it won't make you feel uneasy, it will feel wonderful and you will enjoy the feelings which will help you to drift down even deeper and deeper to a really deep sound sleep. All you want to do is just go on sinking further and further d-o-w-n, drifting d-e-e-p-e-r with every easy breath you take. You're resting quietly and peacefully and nothing will disturb you. You will find this feeling of rest, of being sleepy and drowsy, becomes more and more pleasant as time goes by. It's just as though you're swirling d-o-w-n, being dragged deeper and deeper, floating peacefully into a deep sound sleep, where nothing at all will disturb you and nothing will worry you and all you'll want to do is just go on resting, getting sleepier and drifting deeper. You will soon find that your breathing will become deeper. Breathing deeper". (Notice at this point how your client's breathing deepens and time your words to match it.) "Deep easy breaths, in --------- and --------- out. Take no notice of this and just continue to rest, breathing deeply and drifting d-o-w-n. Any noises you hear will seem such a long, long way off, they will not interest you at all, you won't be interested in anything at all except drifting deeper and deeper to sleep".

(If any noises do occur, you can use these to your advantage by saying something like. "As you hear the sound of the dog barking" or "as you hear the sounds of the cars passing outside, they are now meaningless and just help you to drift even further and further down. All the noises seem such a long, long way off". This will be an advantage if any unforeseen noises do occur.)

"You have learned now how to let go completely. Just let go completely and sink down further getting heavier and heavier. Soon you will start to feel even more comfortable and warm, feeling too tired to bother about anything at all. You may feel a little dizzy or dreamy while I'm talking, or my voice may seem to drift away at times, but take no notice of this, for steadily and quietly you are sinking further and further down even deeper, all the time".

Providing you have followed the correct guidelines without rushing, your client should now be in a deep enough state of hypnosis to respond to further suggestions which will deepen the state even further. Any number of the following routines can be included or you can formulate your own to suit particular individuals. Avoid at all costs, any suggestions which your client would have a fear or resistance to, for example, imagining the sound of the sea if there is a fear of water or having the sunshine beating down on the body if your client burns very easily. It is far better to use ideas which your client would normally find pleasant.

"I will now count from ten to one and as I count I want you to imagine you are walking down a staircase. Any staircase. One step with each number. With every step you take, you will find yourself being dragged even deeper to sleep and becoming heavier. Ten, starting to walk down the staircase. Nine, getting heavier with every step. Eight, falling deeper and deeper with each step you take. Seven, sleepier and sleepier as you walk down the staircase. Six, drifting deeper and deeper. Five, heavier and heavier. Four, sleepier and sleepier. Three, almost at the bottom. Two, relaxing even deeper and One, deeply sound asleep. Now you've reached the bottom of the staircase and in front of you is another. You will walk down this staircase and this time, as you walk down, with every step you take, you will fall twice as deeply to sleep and double your relaxation, with every step. Ten, doubling your relaxation with every step. Nine, falling twice as deeply asleep with every step." etc.

The staircase routine can be repeated as many times as you wish as it will help to deepen the trance, but do not allow it to become too boring. Once you have taken your subject down the flights of stairs, it is a good opportunity to expand on this by explaining that at the bottom of the last flight there is a door which is to be approached and opened. As they open the door you continue with:

"Now you have opened the door and in front of you there is your own private place of paradise. It is the place of your dreams and the place you have longed to visit. This is now your very own private place where there is nobody else and you have total freedom to do anything you like. Then continue. "As you enter your own private place of paradise you feel totally at ease, you can feel the soft golden sand on your feet and between your toes. The warm summer sun is beating down on your body and it feels wonderful. The leaves of the palm trees are gently rustling in the warm summer breeze and the birds are singing in the distance. The sweet fragrances of the flowers are drifting over the cliffs and you can hear the sound of the sea gently licking and lapping up and down the shoreline".

Continue with suggestions similar to these and observe the reactions. It is then a suitable time to start your suggestion therapy explained later.

When you have deepened the trance partially (to the point where your client is entering the paradise beach), you should change your music to a subliminal sounds recording. As I have already mentioned, the more senses you bring into operation the better and you will now see the benefits of the "outside influences", for example the trance will be deepened even further when you say: "as you walk along the golden sand etc……… hear the birds singing………. smell the sweet fragrances of the summer flowers…………. hear the sound of the sea gently licking and lapping up the shoreline………." Your client will indeed associate the warmth of the room with summer, they could imagine birds singing on the subliminal tape, they will smell the Lavender and Frankincense as summer flower fragrances and definitely hear the sound of the sea. Take as long as you feel necessary for this part, it is extremely enjoyable for the hypnotised person.

Always remember to give safety device instructions before you start by saying "Before we start the session, if for any reason during the therapy, your immediate attention is required, you will instantly become wide awake and alert to deal with any situation presented to you."

Do not actually state colours, types of birds or actual fragrances as this may cause conflict and confusion in their mind if they are thinking about something else e.g. You say red roses when they may be thinking of highly scented honeysuckle. – Leave it open ended and entirely up to their own imagination.

Time your talking and breathing to coincide with theirs. Use the words "deeper, relaxing, sleepier, heavier etc" on their out breath and stretch them out and don't forget that counting down helps relaxation while counting up tends to help awaken. Your client should now be in a suitable state to accept suggestions. Look for the physical indications explained earlier.

STANDARD PHRASES FOR HYPNOTIC INDUCTIONS

"The deeper you go the better you will feel, and the better you feel, the deeper you will go to sleep."

"With every breath you take, every noise you hear, every word I say and every thought that you think, you'll go deeper and deeper to sleep."

"Every muscle in your body from the tips of your toes to the tips of your fingers, now becoming so limp, so loose and so relaxed."

"Each and every muscle in your body, now becoming so heavy and so tired."

"Your eyelids are feeling so heavy and so tired, in fact, the harder you try to keep them open, the more they want to close tightly, as you relax completely."

"As you sit (or lie) there in the comfortable chair, it almost feels as though every movement would be a great effort, as though you are sinking down deeply into the chair and into calm, satisfying, relaxation."

"This feeling of warmth and relaxation, is now travelling around your entire body and as you continue to breathe deeply and regularly, you are drifting deeper and deeper to sleep."

"All the worries, stresses and tensions of days gone by, are leaving your mind and leaving your body now, allowing you to relax completely."

"Just as your subconscious makes you breathe at night, or circulates the blood around your body, in just the same way you can faithfully rely upon your subconscious mind to help you eliminate this problem from your every day life."

"It becomes habit in your subconscious mind to smoke (or whatever) and now your subconscious mind will make it habit not to smoke (or whatever)"

"Something that you thought would be difficult to achieve will turn out to be ridiculously easy to do."

"Each morning when you awake, from this moment forward, you will awaken with an inner warm glow of confidence, a renewed optimism to life and a more positive attitude to get things done."

"Every day, in every way, things will be getting better and so much easier to cope with."

"You have made a promise to yourself to (whatever) and whilst it may be alright, on occasion, to break a promise to a friend, your subconscious mind will not allow you to break a promise to yourself and, as such, success is guaranteed."

NOTE: I hope these above examples will give you a much better idea of how therapy room suggestions should be worded for maximum, positive effect. Common sense and a little thought is all you require to word your own suggestions. Just remember the golden rule, that there must never be any doubt in their mind of what you want them to do.

PART EIGHT

SOME EXAMPLE SCRIPTS

There now follows four examples of suitable suggestion therapy for clients with some of the most popular complaints, smoking (this can be easily adapted for other habits), weight loss, confidence with other people and skin complaints. The suggestions should be given when your client has been taken into the deepened state.

STOPPING SMOKING

"All the outside sounds will continue, but they are not important now and you will take no notice of anything except the sound of my voice. Just centre your attentions on the suggestions which I will give you. Nothing can distract you and nothing will disturb you while you are listening. Peacefully and feeling wonderfully calm and relaxed in your own private place of paradise. All the time drifting deeper and deeper while you listen to the sound of my voice. All the suggestions will help you, they are for your benefit. No one is making you stop smoking, you are stopping because you want to and you know it makes sense. Some people resent having to stop smoking and feel irritable, this is because they don't really want to stop or they don't think that they should. But you are different, because you have now decided that you really do want to stop and you now have the will and desire to stop smoking with no feelings of resentment or irritability. In fact, you will feel much, much better for stopping. You will feel cleaner and healthier. You feel very happy and glad you have made up your own mind to stop smoking. You feel relieved to be free of a weed and you are proud of the fact that you are no longer a slave to the drug of nicotine. You are now released from the grip of cigarettes for ever and you feel a wonderful sense of personal achievement. Now that you are an adult, you know that you don't have to prove to anybody that you are an adult by smoking as you may have done in the past as a child. You no longer need to prove that you are a man/woman by smoking, in fact people will now respect you more for not smoking and really admire you for stopping. You may have used to smoke because it seemed to give satisfaction, but it has not been very satisfactory at all, has it (slight pause). The smell and taste of tobacco is unpleasant and if you get smoke in your eyes it stings and causes tears to come. If you enter a room where many people are smoking, your eyes sting and your clothes and hair absorb the nasty smell. You may also find that you cough as a result of tobacco smoke. All these unpleasant side effects will now disappear because you have stopped and your lungs will start to recover. This makes you feel even more proud of yourself. If you have tried to stop smoking before, you may have had withdrawal symptoms and found it unpleasant to stop or were continually thinking of how you wanted a cigarette. You now know that you are doing this in an entirely different way. You have stopped smoking altogether by using hypnosis and the very powerful help of your subconscious mind. Your subconscious mind is your inbuilt computer and is accepting all the helpful suggestions to store and use in the future. This part of your mind knows that it is bad for you to smoke. That is why you have stopped. You are now a very proud non smoker. Another reason you have decided to stop is to save money. If you smoke 20 cigarettes a day for 40 years it will cost you £40 000. Just think what you could spend that money on. You will now save all that money for yourself and your family. It is a great relief to know that you no longer smell of tobacco, that your breath is fresh, that your clothes are clean and free of the smell and ash, your fingers are unstained and your teeth are whiter. You will also taste your food much better and your skin tone will improve. You will have more energy and be able to sleep better. Now, with every deep breath you take, drifting even deeper, you are becoming more and more determined not to let tobacco get hold of you again. With every day that passes, you will become more and more determined to remain a non smoker and be proud of it. Now that you are a non smoker and your food will taste better, you will be aware of this, but will be careful to eat properly. You will only eat enough food to give you the amount of energy that you require and no more that you eat now. Your appetite is fully satisfied with the same amount of food as before. Now (name of client), you will leave here as a non smoker and we are both very, very confident that you will have no need to smoke ever again. You will have no reason or desire ever again. Never, never at any point, will you have the desire to smoke because you will have an extremely positive attitude. You will have no negative thoughts, they will all be positive and further strengthen your resolve. Sometimes, when people attempt to give up without help, they tend to think "oh dear, suppose I get withdrawal symptoms, or suppose I miss smoking," That is a negative attitude, it is just in the mind. Your mind can create any symptoms it wants and negative attitudes can be thought in the imagination. You will have a very positive attitude which will help you. Now (name of client), I want you to go even deeper now, relaxing further, five, deeper, four, deeper and deeper, three, that's right, doing very well even deeper, two relaxing deeper, and one, so deep, very well done. I now want you to imagine that someone in the room has lit a cigarette. See that cigarette, long, white, with filter tip and see the smoke rising from the lighted end. You know that if the smoke got into your nose, you would hate it, it would sting and be uncomfortable. Now (name of client), that cigarette is under your nose, you can smell it, you can sense it when you breathe, you will feel stinging and unpleasant smells from the smoke and you don't like it. If ever you are tempted to smoke again you will remember this and you will know it will make you feel uneasy and perhaps sickly. To get rid of this nasty smoke I want you to say these words quietly to yourself, under your breath for only you to hear. REPEAT. "I never want to smoke again, I want clean fresh air." Repeat this to yourself and the feelings will go away and you will feel fine. See how much better that feels now. You feel good again now and you like yourself and are proud of yourself. You like yourself because you have done this for yourself. You brought yourself here and you are happy that you did. You feel really special. You are going to leave here with a positive attitude and your mind will not create withdrawal symptoms, but will just help you to remain peaceful and calm. This will enhance and reinforce your determination. You are co-operating very well, you are doing excellent, allowing the access to your subconscious mind where there is no resistance. All the time you are helping to increase your determination to remain a non smoker. You are now feeling really very good about yourself, just as if a heavy weight has been lifted off your shoulders and you can start a new healthier life with your family. You will not miss or pine for cigarettes and you won't feel deprived. Cigarettes are not worth missing or worth caring about. That's why you feel good and pleased with yourself. You have not lost anything but you have gained a great deal. You will have more money, your children will be happier and safer, you will not have nicotine stained fingers, your house will smell better and your breath will be fresher. When you see someone else smoking it will not give you the desire to smoke. It will have opposite effect on you and will strengthen your resolve. You will feel sorry for that person who is smoking and will want to help them, but you can't, they've got to help themselves, just as you have done by coming here. You will be glad that you are not doing to yourself what they are doing and what you used to do to yourself. You are now looking forward very much to the rest of today as a non smoker and your husband/wife will notice this too. They will be full of admiration of you and tomorrow when you wake up to a whole new day when all thoughts of smoking will be dismissed totally out of your mind you will feel wonderful as a non smoker. You won't want to even think about smoking, you will prove to your family and friends that it is easy with the help of hypnotherapy. You just want to breath pure healthy air. And any time you like, you can close your eyes and remember your own special phrase which you say under your breath to yourself which is: "I never want to smoke again, clean fresh air." Say it to yourself again. You have now successfully broken the habit and you are well and truly a non smoker. You do not smoke any more. So soon I am going to wake you up and when I do you will feel an overwhelming feeling of being very, very healthy. You will be determined never to smoke again, you will be glad you are now a non smoker and proud of the fact. You will never again smoke another cigarette. When you wake up you will have an overwhelming feeling of being very, very healthy. You will be determined never to smoke. You will be happy and feel fine, alert and full of energy and vitality.

One – Determined never to smoke again.
Two – Feel very healthy and starting to wake up
Three – Waking up further feeling happy and confident
Four – Feeling full of energy, vitality
Five – Wide awake feeling fine.

WEIGHT LOSS

"All the outside sounds continue around you and you are still in your place of paradise but the outside sounds are not important now. Just centre your attention on these suggestions which will help you. Nothing can distract you or disturb you while you are listening to my voice. Drift deeper and deeper while you are listening. These suggestions will help you. They are for your benefit. No one is making you loose weight, you are doing it for yourself. You really want to loose weight and you will do it with a positive attitude which you now have. You are now ready to let go of the excess pounds which you no longer want or need. You are letting go of the excess weight easily and effortlessly. Your appetite is getting smaller and smaller. It is just as if your stomach has shrunk a little and simply cannot take in as much food as it used to. You feel lighter and freer with every day, loosing the excess pounds one by one and it's so easy. You only eat modest portions of food and you are satisfied, completely satisfied. You do not eat between meals, you never eat between meals and you can already see yourself in front of the full length mirror, wearing those clothes which you longed to be able to get into and you look wonderful. Just see yourself there. It fits you perfectly. You look great, light and free. If ever you are tempted to overeat you will close your eyes, take a deep breath and say the words, slim and trim, slim and trim. Repeat these words to yourself now, under your breath. Slim and Trim. Whenever you are tempted to overeat you will close your eyes, take a deep breath and say slim and trim. You will concentrate on your food, notice the colours, notice the textures, you will eat each piece slowly, chew each mouthful slowly and thoroughly, think about what you are eating. You do not eat fatty food. You do not like fatty food. You eat only lean, healthy food and eat it slowly and deliberately. See yourself as slim and healthy. You are becoming more vibrant as your eating habits become healthier. You eat your food slowly. Chew slowly. Enjoying your food. Enjoying the different textures, the clean fresh taste of healthy food. You slowly eat your food and see yourself as vibrant and healthy. You are learning to eat only healthy food and you are becoming pleased with yourself. You like the new slimmer person that you are becoming. You are beginning to loose weight and you are aware that other people are starting to see you as trim and attractive. This makes you feel happy and even more determined to carry on eating only good healthy food. Each day as you loose pounds and inches, your interest in life becomes greater. The more you enjoy life, the healthier and happier you become. You only eat the food you need and you will not eat more than your body needs. You will not eat between meals. As your body burns up the excess fat, your skin becomes clearer and more youthful looking. Your body fat is melting away, leaving you looking and feeling younger and firmer and more dynamic. If you go out for a meal, you choose food which is only low in fat. You eat slowly and only as much as your body needs. As your body fat melts away you are becoming more interesting as a person. People like to meet you and you are enjoying the new attention you are drawing amongst others. This makes you happy and more determined to eat less and burn up even more body fat. You will loose weight regularly every week until you are at your desired body weight and you will like yourself. You like the new slim trim body that is developing with your new eating habits. You have totally lost the desire to eat snacks between meals. Your 2 or 3 small meals a day are sufficient for your body's needs and you look good. The new slim trim figure you are developing is healthy, firm, vibrant and full of energy. You will never again eat more than you need. You have lost all the desire to eat stodgy, fatty foods. You have lost all desire to eat unhealthy foods. You have lost all desire to eat between meals. The new slim you is emerging like a butterfly from a crysalis becoming firm, healthy and full of energy. You will stay firm, trim and full of energy. You will never again overeat. You will start your new eating habits from today. From today you will restructure your life and start your new eating habits. You will not let yourself or anyone else down. You will stick strictly to your reduced food intake. You will enjoy the wonderful adventure of getting slimmer and slimmer and seeing the scales going down every week. Just see yourself on those scales now with them registering your ideal weight and see and feel how good it feels. You will get down to your own target weight in a positive manner and you will enjoy feeling good about it. Now see yourself in a full length mirror at your ideal weight and wearing your ideal clothes which you want to wear, maybe in your swimwear or the glamorous dress you long to wear. See yourself there and feel how good it is. Each week that goes by you will become slimmer and slimmer. You will find that your appetite gets smaller and smaller and that you are satisfied with far less food than you used to be. In a few moments I will wake you up and when I do you will feel an overwhelming desire to carry out all the suggestions which have been made. When you wake up you will be absolutely determined to loose the weight and you will feel happy and confident about it. I will wake you up by counting from 1 to 5 and when I do you will feel very refreshed, confident, happy full of vitality and determined.

One – Starting to wake

Two – Feeling refreshed, confident
Three – Eyes opening, feeling happy, full of vitality
Four – Waking up feeling confident about loosing weight
Five – Wide awake feeling fine.

SKIN PROBLEMS

Now (name of client) I want you to go to your own private place of paradise, where the birds are singing beautiful songs, the wonderful scent of summer flowers fill the air. There are palm trees with their leaves gently rustling in the warm breeze. You can see and hear the sea gently licking and lapping up the coastline. You will walk down 5 steps to your place of paradise and then along the soft warm golden sand. Walk down the steps and count yourself down going deeper all the time. Walk along the beach without a care in the world. You are totally safe because there is no one else around for miles. Feel the soft sand on your feet and between your toes and enjoy it. You are now free from the rest of the world and you have no cares or worries. See yourself there. See yourself in the warm sunshine. There is not a cloud in the sky, there is nobody about, you can hear the birds singing, smell the beautiful flowers, hear the sea, the palm trees are around you with their leaves gently rustling above. You are there and you can see yourself with soft, healthy, clear skin. There is not a blemish on your body and you feel good, you feel happy and confident. You feel really good and proud of yourself without a blemish on your body. Tell me what you are doing now. Tell me what you are wearing.

You are hearing subliminal messages to your subconscious mind which will help you beat your stress and worry. You will have healthy, clear skin as you are now determined to overcome the psoriasis which used to upset you but does not any more. You have now learned to remove your stress by allowing your body to heal it for you. You know you are a very special person and very important. To heal your psoriasis all you have to do is relax, take a deep breath and say to yourself "I am healing myself" REPEAT.

When you say these words you will feel your whole body tingling which is the sign that your adrenaline and beneficial chemicals are being released and starting to attack and destroy your psoriasis. Keep saying these words to yourself and feel the pleasant tingling in your whole body starting to move to all the areas of your psoriasis and destroy it. You can already feel it reducing. The more you say these words to yourself the stronger the attack on the psoriasis will become until it has no further resistance and gives in and disappears altogether. All through this you will feel pleasantly happy that the psoriasis is being removed. You will remain totally calm and relaxed throughout the process. Keep saying to yourself "I am healing myself" REPEAT and feel the wonderful sensations. You may be wondering when your psoriasis will go altogether, but it will. You will remain happy, calm and relaxed throughout. You will remember this place of paradise and every day you will be able to relax and count from 10 to 1 and say to yourself. "I am healing myself" REPEAT until the tingling starts and moves to attack the areas of psoriasis. You are calm and happy throughout this. You will easily be able to remember this place of paradise always, but when you relax yourself and count backwards from 10 to 1 you will be there and feel very good. And as you say your special phrase to yourself "I am healing myself" and keep repeating it, the tingling will start and then move through your body to attack and remove you psoriasis. And you will feel wonderful. In a few moments I will wake you up by counting from 1 to 5 and when I do you will have an overwhelming feeling of well being in body and mind, you will feel refreshed and alert. You will be very very positive and confident about hypnotherapy and will be very eager to experience them for your benefit and speed up the clearing of your skin very soon and these feelings will stay with you.

I will wake you up by counting from 1 to 5

One – Feeling an overwhelming sense of well being in both body and mind
Two – Feeling very positive and confident about hypnotherapy.
Three – Wanting to speed up clearing your skin
Four – Waking up further starting to feel refreshed and alert
Five – Wide awake feeling wonderful and happy.

The above script should be suitably modified for the individual concerned. Encourage your client to use the self hypnosis techniques and listen regularly to the audio cassette you provide. The levels of physical and mental relaxation involved sometimes will result in cure themselves.

CONFIDENCE BUILDING WITH OTHER PEOPLE

"All the outside sounds continue, but they are not important now. You won't be interested in anything except drifting down, even deeper, while listening to my voice. All the suggestions will help you. They are for your benefit. No one is forcing you to tackle and your problems. You have now decided that you are doing it for yourself and with the immense power of your unconscious mind, you will easily be able to beat the memories and negative thoughts you were holding. You are now going about this in a totally different way with only positive thoughts and a confident approach and you know this will help you succeed. This new adventure in your life will reap tremendous rewards. From now on, and with every day that passes, you will be filled with confidence and have a very positive attitude with every new challenge in front of you. Each and every time you meet new people, whether they are male or female, you will have a warm comforting feeling inside of supreme self confidence. You will remain calm and relaxed at all times, just as you are now and you will not allow your mind to play tricks on you. You will have no negative thoughts at all. All your thoughts will be positive and satisfying. You will remain calm and relaxed whenever you are due to meet new people. The negative thoughts and memories you used to have will be totally dismissed and your new, positive way of thinking will carry you through with pride and self satisfaction. The negative thoughts and memories you once had will be totally dismissed, as that is all they are – memories – and they don't matter any more. The only thing which matters now is moving forward and a positive, confident manner. Your unconscious mind is there to help you and it will help you in the future. It will allow you to dismiss, from this day forward, all negative past memories and replace them with wonderful positive thoughts and desires. At any time in the future, you will be able to engage the help of your unconscious mind to help you in any situation or any circumstance. At any time in the future, you will be able to simply close your eyes, take a deep breath and say these words to yourself: Calm, peaceful, tranquil. Calm, peaceful, tranquil. Repeat these words to yourself now and see how good it feels, filling your entire body and mind with a warm confidence. As you keep repeating these words to yourself, you will feel a pleasant warm sensation which calms your whole body and mind and you will feel much better and full of new confidence. You will be able to speak normally, in a calm and reassuring way. You will remain in full control of any situation and will be so calm and positive that people will notice this. People will like and admire you. You will also be proud of yourself and like yourself. People will associate and communicate with you better because they will like your conduct and attitude. They will see you as calm and relaxed and they will appreciate these new qualities. At any time in the future, you will be able to close your eyes, take a deep breath and say the words: Calm, peaceful, tranquil. Calm, peaceful, tranquil. Now repeat these words again to yourself until the warm comforting feelings of confidence move through your body even more. Now just for a moment, imagine yourself in a situation where you are about to meet someone new, but this time you have a totally different approach. You have made your preparations with your keywords and you are totally at ease.”

At this point, take your client, in detail, through a suitable situation in their imagination while meeting a new person, but with the new feeling of confidence and calmness (this is a very powerful technique).

“Now, in a few moments I am going to wake you up and when you wake up, you will remember all the positive suggestions I have given you and you will also remember the wonderful feelings of warm self confidence inside. You will remember all this and keep it to use at any time in the future. When you wake up, you will also feel happy, confident, refreshed, revitalised and relaxed. You will be looking forward to the rest of today and even more so to tomorrow and each further day that passes as your confidence will grow stronger and stronger”.

One – Full of confidence, getting stronger and stronger.

Two – Feeling positive, relaxed and happy

Three – Feeling revitalised and waking a little more.

Four – Determined to continue building, eyes starting to open

And Five – Wide awake, feeling fine.

HYPNO-ANALYSYS

Hypno-analysis is used to help clients with various problems and can sometimes uncover the reasons behind certain fears and phobias.

The technique is relatively simple. You induce the state of hypnosis by which ever method you prefer then suggest to them that "We are going on a journey back in time etc." You can be as inventive as you wish in this and with time and experience will decide which suits you best.

You can simply say "I want you to think back to your childhood. I want you to remember something, anything that happened when you were very young." Do not put ideas or suggestions into their mind by saying something like "Somebody touched you". This would be leading their thinking process. Just ask your client to think back to their childhood days. (You will realise by the end of this course that the majority of neuroses have their roots in childhood and this is why therapists are so interested in the formative years.)

Another way of helping a client to trace their thoughts back is to say, "Think about your final year at school. Think of your teacher's name, think of some of your fellow pupils name." This will almost always awaken a few memories. Then move to the last but one year at school and repeat the technique. Carry on going back through the years as far as you can (unless some important memories come out through the journey backwards) In some cases, a new and possibly startling unpleasant memory may pop out from the unconscious mind giving you material to work on later (this is covered later in psychotherapy).

A further alternative would be to ask your client to free-associate. For this you just tell them to say the first thing that comes into their mind, then the next thing and the next and so on. Instruct your client firmly, not to be selective and not to overlook a thought if they think it may be irrelevant. They must tell you every thought that comes into their mind. Getting a person to freely associate is quite difficult because they usually feel self conscious about it. This is where your previous work with rapport will help.

If you achieve an abreaction in your client, they will probably go into a panic state, but don't let that put you off. They will come to no harm if you show that you are in control. Should your client become distressed in any way you should do the following:

Tell them to relax and assure them that everything is all right and that they are not really in this situation or period in time. They are looking at an image on a large screen, as if at the cinema, and they are totally safe, with you, in the consulting room. All they are doing is acting as an observer of what they are seeing on the screen, they are totally safe and just telling you what they see and hear.

The reason some therapists use Hypno-analysis is establish a point in time which could be relevant to a problem in their present life. For example, someone with a fear of water may in the past have experienced an unpleasant situation with water years ago but are unable to remember anything about it. This is because the memory may have been repressed into the subconscious mind. Hypno-analysis can sometimes be used to take the client back to this point in time and then come to realise what the root cause of the problem is, which can then be part of the cure as they realise why.

Once the situation or problem has been uncovered some clients may be cured immediately. Others will require discussions and counselling sessions to help them come to terms with the outcome. Never leave the opened can of worms unattended with anyone who is not cured as this can be just as psychologically damaging as not treating the problem in the first place.

The principal of Hypno-analysis can be combined with suggestion therapy for smoking, nail biting etc by taking the client back to the point in time when they did not smoke etc. and letting them experience how much healthier they felt.

CREATIVE VISUALISATION

Creative visualisation can be an excellent supplement to suggestion therapy with cases where there are physical symptoms or depression and stress are present. The treatment consists of putting your client into hypnosis and then using the powerful visualisation technique to increase or decrease the symptoms.

Instruct your client to imagine a large side control in front of them set in the middle (similar to a volume slide control adjuster) and that when the control is pushed upwards, the symptoms or pain increases and when it is pushed down they decrease. Tell your client to push the control upwards slowly to a point where the symptoms or pain become almost unbearable. Then tell them to slide the control downwards until the pain or symptoms improve or disappear. This should be practised every day for two weeks and each time the control be moved further downwards until the symptoms disappear completely. If the symptoms should then ever appear again in the future, they should go through the self hypnosis routine and progressively slide the control downwards until improvement is obtained.

ADVANCED HYPNOTHERAPY

With the knowledge you have so far, you should be more than capable of treating the more simple problems such as smoking, confidence, weight loss, nail biting etc. as these lend themselves well to straightforward suggestion therapy. This should be adequate for treating up to 90% of your clients, but as a competent practitioner, you should be able to deal also with the more lasting and deep seated problems.

This involves the principal of psychotherapy and requires the art of counselling and often a great deal of patience. You should, at all times, carry your own belief into your practice that you can help, if not totally cure, any condition which is presented to you. It is much better to hold too positive rather than negative attitude.

Never at any time though claim you can cure things which the medical doctors cannot. This course does not teach the skills of a medical practitioner and you should not attempt to make people believe you are. You will gain more respect both from clients and members of the medical world by portraying yourself as a "Complementary Therapist" rather than an "Alternative Therapist". This way you will be seen as an asset rather than a rival as a "Holistic Practitioner".

<u>**PART NINE**</u>

"BITZ 'N' BOBS"

A CHAPTER OF GENERALLY VERY USEFUL KNOWLEDGE

This chapter has no particular format at all, that's the way I intended it to be. By having no format, you will have to put your own mind to work more to see the truth of what I'm saying and teaching to you, so here goes.

Always remember, that positive thoughts breed positive actions, as they are contagious, and positive actions bring positive success. To be a successful hypnotist, you must have an attractive personality. This personality is a sum total of your health, appearance, habits and attitude. This type of personality is a plus personality, and a plus means that something is added. Negative, is an away sign and you cannot possess negative qualities and be successful. Therefore, any negative qualities you possess must be removed.

Keep healthy, reasonable hours, eat good wholesome food, keep clear of colds, no over indulgence and treat others as you would sincerely expect to be treated yourself. Then you will develop for yourself a magnetic personality. Also remember, that it is vital to master self control, as you will never successfully control others if you cannot control yourself. This point is often overlooked, except by the successful few. Strive always to be healthy in mind, body and soul. You may have some negative attitudes or nervous habits, which must be eliminated, if so strive to get rid of them rapidly. Cut pride and any desire to be important, this is not easy when you know that you have the secret for success, which by the end of this course you will have.

Keep this secret to yourself, but ensure that you carry out the formula. You must master your negative desires, before you can possibly hope to master others. Listen with respect, to the views of others, and always find the good in what is expressed. Do not try to show that you know more about the subject, even if this is the case. People who do this have very poor self control. Never interrupt with objections, better that you spend time saying what is good about the discussion. You will always gain more influence over others by giving credit for what is good and very intelligent. Agreement, more often expressed makes and keeps friends, you just forget the rest, it is better to do so than disagreeing, the latter is negative and to you a loss. So in future, observe the things that you do wrong. Unconsciously these are bad habits, done with little or no conscious thought, they are your disabilities now and they have to be corrected.

The way that your personality comes across in the consulting room is a most important part or heart of any hypnotherapist. Confidence, directness, assertiveness, being totally positive in everything that you do, are all very vital qualities that you need to develop for your career to be a success. You must be able to confidently force your personality, in a non aggressive way, onto your clients.

When counting for relaxation or sleep, count downwards, ie. 5,4,3,2,1, and when terminating the state count upwards, 1,2,3,4,5, etc., so that you are doing the opposite thing, it has the opposite result.

Another clever technique to use during the induction process is to say to the client, "OK, just take a nice deep breath in (the word in being drawn out), hold it and then out (the word out being drawn out)". The words in and out are drawn out to coincide with the client's inwards and outwards breathing rhythm. This has the effect of verbally "mirroring" their breathing rhythm and helps to establish a stronger rapport. This then allows the client to relax more and as such the trance state sets in.

Another general rule of thumb, I have found, is this; when the client breathes out (in other words, on the out breath), it is the best time to suggest things such as, sleep, deeper, relax etc. Psychologically, people associate breathing outwards with letting go and relaxation, and this is the best time to suggest such things.

There are several different states of hypnosis which it is possible for everyone to enter. There are five states of hypnosis, and these are:

THE WAKING STATE (HYPNOIDAL STATE)

This is a lovely lazy state that we all drift into prior to sleep or, although fully conscious, just before we wake up.

THE LIGHT TRANCE (LETHARGIC)

This is the next level of hypnosis, and in this light trance, as the title suggests, the person feels quite lethargic. A flickering of the eyelids is often noticed or a movement of the eyeballs under the lids (known as R.E.M.'s, Rapid Eye Movements). This merely shows that the client is entering a deeper level of trance.

THE MEDIUM STATE (CATALEPTIC TRANCE)

In this state, the person feels detached from their surroundings and very often has a hazy recollection of events when the hypnotic state is ended. This state will cause you no problems, as the client will still respond to your suggestions.

THE DEEP STATE (SOMNAMBULSTIC)

This state is an absolute nightmare for you in your role as a hypnotist. The reason for this being, in this state, they will be enjoying hypnosis so much, that they will want to be left alone.

THE POST HYPNOTIC STATE

I prefer to call this an eye open trance state, as even with their eyes open, in this state you can suggest more things to them and they will immediately react.

SPECIAL NOTE

The only other state after somnambulism is the COMOTOSE state, which as the name suggests resembles the state of coma. To get someone into this state takes a lot of trance deepening and will not even bother you upon the stage.

IDENTIFYING THE TRANCE SUBJECTS ARE IN

The oldest known, and most mentioned scale of hypnotic susceptibility, or scale for measuring the trance state depth, is the Davis/Hubard scale of hypnotic susceptibility. Another scale is that of Leoron/Bordeaux, and both of these can be obtained from any good book store, contained within the pages of various hypnotherapy literature. I will not mention them here, as to be honest, 95% of the population are most likely to go into a light (lethargic) trance. Of the population as a whole, only 55% are likely to enter the medium trance. As for the somnambulistic trance, only about 20% of the population can enter it. Should this occur during your therapy session, you will be able to verbally guide your client back into the state required.

HYPNOTISABILITY OF THE ENTIRE POPULATION

5% Unable to be hypnotised
95% Light trance, the majority of people can participate in your show.
55% Medium trance, Cataleptic.
20% Deep trance, Somnambulistic

I will briefly mention a few of the indications which suggest when a person is in hypnosis. These listed here are the ones I most commonly find. Once you're experienced it will become second nature almost to spot these things which indicate the hypnotic state. For now, here are the main ones to spot.

THE FACIAL FLUSH

The skin tone colour changes as the hypnotic relaxation sets in.

EYELIDS FLICKERING

Eyelid flickering indicates the onset of trance, or a deeper level of trance.

WHITES OF THE EYES

You will notice with some clients, that their eyes have floated upwards behind their lids. There is no cause for concern, if you observe the whites of their eyes through their slightly parted lids; in fact, it just means they are certainly in a trance.

EYES REMAIN OPEN

If this occurs, but the person is actually in trance, then there will be a kind of glazed look upon them. In this case just close their eyelids gently with your fingertips.

THE SCRATCH

Some clients may begin repeatedly scratching themselves on various parts of their anatomy. Don't worry, carry on, they do not consciously realise they are doing it.

QUASIMODO RESPONSE

Some clients, as they relax, will distort their features into the most laughable of unpleasant shapes. This is an involuntary action and they are unaware of it occurring.

OBVIOUS RELAXATION

If their heads fall forwards, or to one side, their jaws sag open, facial and bodily features relax etc., then the suggestions of relaxation, which you have been giving, are influencing the motor actions of their body.

CATATONIC STATE

Sometimes this occurs without suggestion. Some or all of the clients' muscles become rigid or stiff. If this occurs of its own accord, try to reverse it with suggestions of muscular relaxation.

SLEEEEEP

With somnambulists they demonstrate all the signs of actual, genuine sleep. However, they are just in a very deep trance. They will not react to you and their speech will be slurred and lazy. You must awaken these people, make sure they are full conscious and return them to the audience.

TIME DISTORTION

When a person is in hypnosis, time distortion is experienced to a factor of two to two and half times. In a rare case or two, it can be the reverse and the odd client thinks it was twice the length of the time it actually took.

ABREACTION'S

Abreaction's, as the name suggests, are abnormal reactions, which are sometimes experienced by a client in trance and you should certainly be aware of this. Abreactions will become a regular occurrence to you in therapy. When under hypnosis, a person relaxes the critical (analytical) area of the mind. The ego switches off, so this can enhance a client's long term memory. If an abreaction did occur, it would just mean that the client had drifted back through their thoughts, back in time to an earlier period in their development. Back into their childhood, the subconscious mind retains within its memory banks, past experiences of traumatic natures, as well as numerous other incidents/events which have long been forgotten. The reason these things are "blocked out" or "repressed", is because as a youngster, they were far too traumatic to deal with, but now, from an adult viewpoint, it would be easier to come to terms with them.

These repressions are often the cause of fears and phobias that the person has. (The phobias become an outward expression of an inward problem). The moment an abreaction occurs and the traumatic event (repression) is released, so the cause of the problem will be removed and as such all the symptoms will disappear. You see the mind is like an electric kettle, when the water becomes too hot and has boiled, the thermostat in the kettle causes it to switch off, so that it does not boil dry. So it is with the mind, that if a young mind experiences an event of a traumatic nature, then it may be too "hot" for that young mind to handle, so their emotions repress that memory and lock it into the subconscious mind. But the person believes they have forgotten it and even, in some cases believes the traumatic event never took place. In fact when they release the repression, people are usually unaware it was there, or that the repressed event ever took place. So, just as it takes emotion for the event to be repressed, it also takes a lot of emotion to release it and that's all an abreaction is, an emotional release of a repressed memory.

The fears or phobias which that person may have been experiencing then stop, as they were created by the hidden problem in order that the client be consciously drawn to finally sort out those fears/phobias, which in turn also ensures that the repressed problem is eventually dealt with.

Although it's very dramatic to witness, the end result for the person it's happening to, is that their life will improve no end, and fears/phobias they once had will now no longer trouble them. So the result of an abreaction is strong, emotional and/or bodily reactions. Now as a therapist, we'd just let them continue experiencing the state, until they came out of trance naturally, as it would in a therapeutic sense, do them tremendous benefit. It is important that you understand about abreactions because you will come across them.

PUBLIC LIABILITY INSURANCE.

Hypnosis is, I've already state several times, a totally harmless state, however, because the effects of it are all in the mind it would be very hard to prove that the ex-subjects are not a result of our hypnosis. We know it's just not the case, they know it's not the case, but if someone did decide to sue you, in a way like this, for psychological damage or making them feel ill, it would then be your problem to defend yourself in court and prove that it was not hypnosis that did it. So unless you are very rich, an incident such as this example, which by the way, is highly unlikely to occur anyway, (but better safe that sorry), would make you bankrupt trying to defend yourself in court. Unless you had taken out suitable public liability insurance, which would then cover you for the costs of legal cases etc.

If you intend to practice in therapy only, the insurance premiums are more easily obtainable and carry far less premiums – around £50 per annum.

PART TEN

PSYCHOTHERAPY

A wise man once said, "It's not so much the psychological knowledge that you have, as quality of respect and empathy that you afford your client, which brings about healing".

When Chad Vara founded the Samaritans, he set up at an office in a church and people would go along and tell him all their troubles and worries. As the word got round, more and more people started to come and see him. He then enrolled some helpers to make tea and coffee for his clients while they waited to see him.

Gradually, he started to notice that his demand of clients was reducing and as further weeks went by he decided to investigate. To his surprise (although very pleased) he found that the people were not intentionally turning their backs on him, but instead were finding just as much help from the tea and coffee makers! These helpers had no training, so they could do little more than listen and unintentionally were giving what the people needed…….a sympathetic ear, their attention and their time. They were providing these "sufferers" with their greatest need…..another human being to listen and care. From this point onwards, Chad Vara developed the phrase, "Don't just do something, sit there."

During you hypnotherapy and psychotherapy sessions, you will need to make your client feel important and worthwhile enough to want to change and to gain their inner permission to stop hurting themselves. You will never be able to <u>make</u> your client change but you can give them the tool of self value and explain that what has happened in earlier life which may have an effect now, is not their fault. With you ability to use hypnosis also, you will be able to direct these facts easily into your client's mind.

Like all mammals, the human being enters the world from the perfect environment – the womb. In the womb there is warmth, sustenance and usually harmony. There is no strange world of anxiety or confrontation.

It is very important for therapists to be aware of the child's way of coping with the world form the very start, as this is where the personality begins to form and also the thinking pattern which may contribute towards a neurosis later in life. For example, the child may become resentful and angry about being handled roughly for crying and so may develop the idea that the world is an uncharitable place from where you get no favours and you have to look after yourself by whatever means you can. Similarly, if the young child is left alone for long periods, it may well develop a very jaundiced view of the world. Not only is human contact vital for a feeling of safety, but it also contributes towards a well balanced personality and thought pattern.

This may appear a little far fetched, but believe me it is often the way the thought patterns and personality can begin to form. The vital formative years of a human are estimated as being up to the age of seven, therefore there are other factors to be taken into account when you try to asses the client in front of you in your consulting room. As a "therapist of the mind" is very similar to being a detective and you should have enough knowledge to start picking up the clues.

Self perception, as I have detailed earlier, is important. The social philosophers, G. H. Mead and C. H. Cooley claimed that a person's view of their own identity comes about as a result of the way which they are regarded by others. We use our imagination to get from others, a perception of ourselves. When you go into your own practice, you will start to meet people who have a rather distorted view of both themselves and their value.

It isn't true that Freud "discovered" the unconscious, but he did develop the focus of the belief that the unconscious controls much of the way we behave because of the dynamic power it possesses. He then went on to call it the "Dynamic Unconscious". The theory he proposed, which is still observed today, was that unpleasant or traumatic events which took place in earlier life (the formative years) are repressed into the unconscious mind, only to express themselves later on in life, often in disguise and sometimes as symptoms of neuroses.

When you think about how vulnerable the human infant really is and consider the fact that at only two or three days old, they are working out methods of how to deal or react to situations, then you will understand why I say that the young child will often repress any painful, frightening or depressing memory. They do not forget these situations, but simply cast them out of the conscious mind and away into the unconscious.

To complicate matters further, as you will find both on stage and in therapy, there is no concept of time in the unconscious. If a repression goes in , say at the age of two, it will stay that age. I ask you to think about that for a little while………………………… A two year old's emotion hitting a person in their twenties or thirties or forties…. No wonder they become ashamed of their neuroses! Add to that, until they have received therapy they don't know where this feeling is coming from and it seems to be attacking them from thin air, I'm sure you'll agree, it's not difficult to appreciate that they think they are literally going out of their mind. What else can they possibly think if they don't know or understand or if it has not been explained to them. It is vital that you explain these things to them, but I believe this is not the final cure.

Some schools of thought argue that to only discover the cause of a neurotic problem is to cure it. I will here and now state that this is definitely not the case. I and a number of fellow therapists would suggest to you that to carry such a belief to your client who desperately needs your help would do more harm than good and could be dangerous. To discover the cause of a neurotic problem is a very good starting point, but you must then explain to your client what you have learned through this section of the course. The cause of the repression, the way the imagination works, how helpless the young human child is, how confusing the world is to us when we are born, how powerful and influential the parents are, repression – how and why it works - All these facts must be driven home (hypnosis can help here) until they become an accepted part of the daily way of thinking.

Always remember though, at the same time, your job is to be "a good listener".

All this may seem a little daunting at this moment, but believe me, when you have successfully completed this course in Complete Mind Therapy you will have so many different assets and abilities, you will impress your clients and fellow therapists who will realise that you have had extensive training and get referrals and recommendations form sources unable to help. Also, at conferences or professional gatherings, you will be in no way left out of touch or out of your depth. Many therapists in practice today have been taught only by narrow one line methods, but you will be head and shoulders in front of them.

The successful hypnotherapist is a masterful psychotherapist, as well as being an efficient craftsman. You should know life, people, society and always try to notice these with one eye on improving your own skills and understanding, then you will be able to make an even greater contribution towards the curing of the client in front of you.

Hypnotherapy and psychotherapy are very valuable aids to the treatment of cases that have not responded well to ordinary medication. I personally feel with my experience, that they will play an ever increasing role in curing both physical and metal conditions and relieve a great deal of human suffering.

We have here, a powerful curing agent. An elderly wise colleague of mine, who had many years experience, once referred to it as "a powerful drug which you can't put in a bottle" and he often said to his clients, "The genie really is now out of the lamp!." How right he was. As you will now becoming to realise, many seemingly "organic" ailments are physical results of a neurosis which can be helped or cured when the mental conflict is resolved. Medical GP's, whether it be consciously or unconsciously, use suggestion in their practice, so why don't we use it in a more organised and methodical manner as a speciality? Well WE do, and very well too.

For example, the trained nurse knows the importance of all the psychological factors in medicine and realises that the mind must be treated as well as the body. This is done by trying to introduce confidence into the patient and providing a cheerful atmosphere. The road to recovery is also treated with positive anticipation. Problems sometimes arise however when the patient visits their Doctor who is desperately short of valuable time to spend with each individual and sends them off with some pills when the root cause of the problem is in the mind. This is where Private Practitioners – and this includes you – are very successful, by giving the client the time they require, even though they are paying private fees for the service. A point here is that, unless you are running an advertisement campaign, it is not a good idea to give anyone free consultations. The reason being is that if they think they have to pay for the service, there is a far greater success rate.

If you remember the principal of the repressed memories coming out later in life you can compare it to a clock which has stopped ticking and in this case you know there is something wrong internally. Using hypnosis and psychotherapy, you can relatively quickly, uncover the neurotic defence mechanism and then effect the cure. In all cases, you need to remove the cause of the anxiety and give your client an insight into the unconscious reasons which are responsible for the symptoms. The sooner your client faces up to the anxiety and fear, the quicker the cure will be.

I will now cover the most common phobia's and then give you idea's of suitable suggestive therapy given for treatment and ultimate removal. Phobia's are exaggerated fears and as such, can be broken down into almost meaningless confusions of the thought patterns. They can usually be seen as rather foolish by the adult after they have been uncovered.

The phobias are considered to be exaggerated fears because they go beyond what we would think of as "reasonable concern" and a "normal sense of precaution". As a rule they are self induced into the unconscious, as explained earlier and as I will show you later, they can easily be removed.

Agoraphobia	Fear of Open Spaces
Claustrophobia	Fear of Enclosed Spaces
Nosophobia	Fear of Disease
Pathophobia	Fear of Suffering
Astraphobia	Fear of Thunder
Monophobia	Fear of Loneliness

Misophobia   Fear of Dirt and Germs
Acrophobia   Fear of Heights (causing vertigo)
Hematophobia Fear of Blood
Ochlophobia   Fear of Crowds
Erythrophobia Fear of Blushing
Zoophobia   Fear of Animals
Xenophobia   Fear of Strangers/Foreigners
Insectophobia Fear of Insects (mostly spiders)
Nyctophobia   Fear or the Dark
Aichmaphobia Fear of Knives
Hamartophobia   Fear of Failure

Every phobia is simply a state of mind and when you have removed the thoughts of fear, you will then also be able to move on to further processes. Overcoming stammering, hesitation, sowing the seeds of success, ambitions etc.

Please remember the phrase on a bottle of pills, "If symptoms persist, consult your doctor". Should you find that the phobic symptoms continue after therapy, you should refer your client for medical or psychiatric advice. There are sometimes (although a very small percentage) cases where there are physical problems and chemical imbalances in the brain which require medical attention. I remember a case of a young woman in her twenties who was pregnant where, because of this, hypnosis was not wise. She had previously been on medication for "depression" and came for therapy as a last resort. (This incidentally is often the case. People often try many, many different methods before they turn to us for a permanent cure). She had an unexplainable inner belief of total mistrust of her husband and was convinced that every other woman was a potential threat to her. She was constantly checking up on him, even at his work which started to get him into trouble. Many of their friends were lost over quite a short period as her accusations started to spread to anyone and everyone. As time went by during the Counseling and Psychotherapy sessions and speaking independently to her husband, it became clear that there was something else which was not quite right. To cut a long story short, after recommending she sought further medical advice, it turned out that the "depression" was actually "acute paranoia" which was caused by chemical deficiencies. A new medication was prescribed which improved the situation no end. This factual example is just to show you that each case should be treated on its own merit, but the majority will respond exceptionally well to your therapy.

Imagine for a moment, a child being forced by its parents to sleep alone in a bedroom while there is a violent thunderstorm outside. In later life, whenever there is a thunderstorm, the adult mind goes back straight away to the terrifying time in that bedroom, all alone, frightened and the fear is relived all over again.

Again, in the early years, a child may have been bitten by a dog or scratched by a cat. In later life there can be a fear of dogs or cats, to have them near would be unbearable and to stroke a cat or fuss a dog would be unthinkable. Both animals could bring back, through association of ideas, the terrifying experience of former years.

As with the thunderstorm and the animals, the relevant phobias set in. This is why you must discover the basic reason for the problem. This as I have mentioned before, is the abreaction – the reacting of an unpleasant experience in order to discover and accept the origin.

To give you some examples of how to tackle phobia's the following guidelines will be helpful. You should obviously use your own common sense and always use the principals of what you have learned so far in the course. The sessions are in a more traditional approach and it is up to you whether you use these methods or the much quicker "30 minute fast phobia cure" method explained later. Both methods are in your course to ensure you have the widest possible knowledge of the subject and as such will be far ahead of many of your future colleagues.

FEAR OF OPEN SPACES

Recall

Were you alone in a large field with a bull? Was there a wind blowing? Were you approached by a stranger? Had you lost your parents? Were you soaking wet in the rain? Did you feel frightened and lonely? Were you lost? Did you become frightened to venture into open spaces? Or were you out in the crowds and become fearful in the busy streets? Did you loose your way? Did anybody frighten or harass you?

These sample questions will start to help your client remember part thoughts until suddenly, the truth will dawn and they will recall the reason that made them fearful of open spaces. There is now apparently a very good reason for being afraid.

Repair

Tell your client what happened then will not happen again in the same way. They are no longer a child. They will not get lost. The wide open spaces and the countryside are wonderful places to be and the trees, grass, flowers, expanses of blue sky are beautiful. When alone in these places, they need have no fear. In crowded streets they are surrounded by many others who are only on their daily business, just as they are. Strangers will not accost them. They are no longer afraid of people walking beside, in front, or behind them or going in and out of shops. They are not afraid of each other. They like the sounds and are no longer afraid of anyone because there is now no reason to be.

FEAR OF ENCLOSED SPACES

Recall

Were you once shut up in a cupboard or other confined space on purpose or by accident? Did you become locked in somewhere and could not get out? Were you frightened somewhere, like the underground with lots of people and felt you could not get out? Were you ever lost in a wood or somewhere similar surrounded by tall trees and could not find your way out? Were you ever trapped in a lift and unable to get help to be released? Have you ever been traveling in a car at high speed and thought you may be in an accident?

These types of questions will alert the past negative experiences which may have contributed to feeling suffocating, closed in or frightening.

Repair

Tell your client that these are only memories of the past. They will never again be locked in and unable to get out. When traveling on the underground, yes, they are surrounded by other people, but they are friendly and they too will feel hot and bothered, but they are talking to each other and they are not afraid. There is no reason why they should be afraid. There is plenty of air. If they are in a fast traveling car, they can open the windows and let air in. The driver is friendly and knows what he/she is doing. It's best to sit back, relax and enjoy the countryside as soon the journey will be over.

FEAR OF HEIGHTS

Recall

Was there a time, in your childhood or youth, when you looked down from a great height and it felt absolutely dreadful? As if you had the feeling you were going to throw yourself down to the ground? Did you have to pull back quickly, as the world started to swim around before your very eyes and you felt you were loosing your balance? Or, perhaps when on holiday or out walking at the weekend, you may have been climbing a hill and looking down, those dreadful feelings of vertigo came over you? Then, if you could not have grabbed a handrail or a tree, the dizziness may have made you fall and plunge to the bottom? Even if you haven't had this actual experience, you may have still got an automatic fear of heights and be unable to get to them without having an attack of vertigo or even worse, feeling you may fall or throw yourself off the ledge or hilltop?

Any number of past memories may be relevant here. Even recalling a horror film.

Repair

Tell your client that this phobia is not only a matter of the mind. It's also a question of the sense of balance dictating to the brain what they see and hear which are connected. Use the Creative Visualisation technique to take your client through the experience, but this time with a new approach and full confidence in a relaxed manner. Keep instilling into them that they can not and will not fall. They have no desire to throw themselves off.

Walk away slightly from the edge and take deep regular breaths until they feel much better.

FEAR OF BLOOD

Recall

Was your first sight of blood that of your own or somebody else's? How did you react at the sight of your own blood? Did it happen as a result of an accident or injury or having a blood test? Did it make you feel faint? Did it cause you to pass out in childhood? If it was the sight of another person's blood because of an accident or an attack, did it make you shudder? Did you have to turn away from the sight? Were you or did you feel sick? Did you find the sight of blood repulsive? If you saw an accident with an animal, did it make you feel the same? Do you now feel frightened of cutting or grazing yourself in case you draw blood? Would you shudder at the thought of having a blood transfusion in hospital? Would you be unable to give blood as a donor?

From the types of questions above, I am sure you will very quickly see how this particular phobia starts.

Repair

Tell your client that blood is the life force of every living human and animal. They may fear the sight of it because it is red which is the colour of anger, war and conflict. They are lucky to have healthy blood and they are not anaemic. Without blood they would not be alive and healthy. Without blood, the people they know and love would not be alive. They should not turn away from the sight of blood at an accident, but they can and must steel their nerves if it means they can help someone who is suffering from blood loss. If, at some time in the future, they require a blood transfusion, they should welcome it, because some donor has given them the chance of life. If they are required to give blood in an emergency, they will feel happy that they are in the privileged position of being able to help save someone's life. If they see an animal in distress, loosing blood, they will do all in their power to help and not turn away in weakness or disgust. If they injure themselves, they will not faint at the sight of their own blood, but will take all necessary steps to remain calm and stem the blood flow without becoming squeamish.

You will now appreciate that, with the power of hypnosis and the correct way of approaching and phrasing things it is quite easy to re-program the negative thought patterns. The remaining phobia's can all be dealt with in a similar manner for a lasting cure.

EIGHT NEGATIVE STATES OF MIND

COVERSION NEUROSIS

A worry turned into an illness

OBSESSIONS

Fixed ideas that cannot be dismissed by common sense.

INFANTILISM

A childish attitude to problems in order to escape finding a solution.

INHIBITIONS

Mental brakes put on normal everyday actions.

COMPULSIONS

Fixed feelings that certain actions must be taken, otherwise you will be in danger or things will go wrong.

ANXIETY NEUROSIS

Unreasonable worry about ordinary things, circumstances and situations.

INTROVERSION

The desire to withdraw from life, from society and family. To always be looking back instead of forward. Living in the past instead of the present and not looking to the future with positive hope.

SCHIZOPHRENIA

The "Jekyll and Hyde" condition. A serious mental illness in advanced cases but, in ordinary everyday ways, a general sense of moodiness and temperament. An up and down outlook which is disconcerting and upsetting.

FURTHER PROBLEMS TO TACKLE AT ADVANCED LEVEL

ACUTE DEPRESSION

Acute depression can strike at any time of life and on any person, but it is more common in women. The reasons for it occurring are too numerous to mention but include repressed memories form childhood, social, domestic or professional problems and even the pressures and pollution of life itself. One thing for sure, is that when this problem presents itself to you, you should treat it with urgency because it is unlikely to improve of its own accord and the consequences could become serious.

Exactly the same principals are used as you have learned, by getting to the root cause of the problem and then breaking the behavioural loop. When this has been established, you should instil feelings of confidence, self worth, esteem and ego as explained earlier. Often an audio cassette provided to use at home gives added benefits.

SEXUAL PROBLEMS

This is an area which could be developed into a full time practice in its own right and you could be a pioneer of this therapy in your own particular area of the country. The one thing to observe here though, is to keep yourself at a sensible distance from your client/s. (On this subject you will often find that you have both the male and female members of the relationship for consultations either at the same or different times). You are **not** a marriage guidance counsellor, you are a therapist and as such should not let yourself become involved in the relationship or even worse, start giving advice on whether one partner should leave the other etc. If you get involved in this, there will always be one side of the relationship which will see you as "wrong" and there will be a come-back which will damage your reputation. It is simply not worth it.

Impotence in the male is relatively easy to deal with, but frigidity in the female can be more deep seated and often requires a little more patient progress.

The Male

In most cases, the failure to achieve and/or retain an erection is only psychological and is exactly the same as the patterns which I have explained earlier. The chances are, that at some time in the past, for whatever reason, the man has failed (as far as he is concerned) to perform satisfactorily due to outside influences such as stress, worry, overwork etc. This then stays with him or reappears later as a fear of failure during sexual intercourse. This is compounded by thinking that he will fail again and again and so he enters the viscous circle. Assuming that he was able before this and has no medical reason why he cannot, then the treatment pattern should follow confidence building and creative visualisation techniques.

While in hypnosis take him through the process in a relaxed, confident manner. Tell him to imagine that he is now the greatest lover. He will be performing so well that everything is perfect and he is giving his partner immense pleasure and satisfaction. His erection will be strong and long lasting and he will be the tentative lover throughout the session. He will be able to make the session last as long as he desires.

All through these suggestions, keep your phrases vibrant and positive which will describe in detail how good things will be for both of them.

There is an important intermediate stage for sexual therapy in the form of counseling advice. This should be aimed at both the male and female and is designed to be psychologically rewarding by denial! This may seem strange to you at the moment, but believe me, the more people are denied of things, the more they want them. This is especially true with the natural human desire of sex.

Tell the couple to specifically put aside a two month period where they should "go back to basics". They should put aside a little time each week to spend with each other wherever and whenever the time suits them. They should start doing the things they used to do. A glass of wine in front of the fire, the lights dimmed down low for a change, a romantic film, taking a bath together and absolutely anything else which takes their fancy. They should kiss, cuddle and caress each other, even to the point of foreplay, but no sexual intercourse. The reason for this is to relieve the pressure on the man and put his mind at rest that from the start, nothing is expected of him sexually. If they observe your recommendations of keeping to this for two months, then they will, almost certainly be soon be enjoying revitalised lovemaking within days of the end of the period.

The Female

Frigidity in the female requires your skills as an all round therapist to effect a cure. The first thing to establish is whether there is a deep seated fear or phobia about sex. You have now learned how to uncover these and how to deal with them. Involve the male partner to enlist his help (for his partner) and thus developing an association and double barreled attack on the problem.

If you establish that there is no real deep seated problem which is contributing to the situation, you should advise a similar pattern as the treatment of the male, but for a slightly longer period, say an extra three to four weeks.

REGRESSION

Regression is sometimes a little controversial as people can sometimes relive or "remember" false memories and although it has been used on many occasions successfully it should be treated with caution. It is a method of taking people back into "past lives" and letting them explain when and where things were happening. Imagine the scene from years ago when you were engrossed in a film or a book and actually felt part of the situation. Then think of how powerful the subconscious mind is and that the memories are stored away in there. Now put yourself into the position of being in some way associated with a *similar* situation and imagine how easy it is to truly believe that you have knowledge of something from the past. This is how easy mistakes can be made.

The subject of regression in depth would warrant a whole course such as this one and therefore the principals only are included to give you a complement to your therapy knowledge. Use it with extreme caution, if at all, and be prepared for unpleasant possible reactions.

The procedure for regression is simply to take your client into the deepened hypnotic trance and then give the following instructions:

"I am now going to take you back in time a little at a time until you reach the point in time you want to reach. You will travel back in time past the point of your birth and into a past life. Don't try too hard, but let it just happen naturally, as I take you back. Just let your mind drift back through time and you will become more and more relaxed. In a moment, I will click my fingers and each time I do, you will travel back in time a little further. One or two years backwards in time with each click of my fingers. Easily and gently you will drift back in time with every click of my fingers. (Click) Going back, back, easily and gently. (Click) Moving further back through the years. (Click) Year by year, drifting backwards through time……." Continue along these lines and then say. "Is it night or day? Are you inside or outside? Are you with others or alone? What is your name? What are you wearing? Who are your friends? Who are your enemies? Are you married or single? Do you have any children? What are their names?

You can be as creative as you like when using regression and gradually build up a picture of where the person is. Recording the session or taking notes will enable you to cross check any information disclosed. If you have an interest in this subject, you will find actual documented accounts of people disclosing accurate information using regression of past lives from various text books available.

Should your client start to become distressed, you should use the same methods described earlier to calm the situation.

SHADOWING TAPES

The "Shadowing Tape" available from your supplier will prove successful for many or indeed all your hypnotic inductions. A shadowing tape played at the same time as your hypnotic induction will add to the relaxation, confusion, disorientation and attention of your client and so enhance the effects.

The principal behind this is that the "attention" is the act of concentration on one or more physical functions or pieces of information which are hitting the senses. When attending to just one piece of information we are being selective, but when we give our attention to more than one source, we are demonstrating divided attention. Some functions need all our attention, while others need only part of our concentrations. Things which we have not properly learned call for a higher level of thought and concentration than routines which we perform as automatic reflex actions. Think back to the riding a bike or driving a car routines I explained earlier.

When we go through familiar routines, we are able to do and say other things at the same time and give only limited or divided attention to the task in hand. It follows therefore, that when your client is being guided into hypnosis, spoken words on a lower level to do with relaxation and sleep will help with the process.

The principal is straightforward. Just record onto an audio cassette simple keywords which are associated with relaxation, sleep, going deeper, feeling heavier, drifting down, feeling comfortable, totally at ease etc. etc. If you like, you can also mix some suitable music at the same time. As you start your induction, you then play this audio cassette at a lower volume than your spoken voice and your client will be picking up these commands to reinforce what you are saying. The example provided is for an induction, but you can record any number for use with different problems and use them as required. Smoking, for example, would have different keywords and would be played during your suggestion therapy.

<u>**PART ELEVEN**</u>

SHORTCUTS TO ALTERNATIVE MEDICINE

This section of the course is purposely presented in a hap-hazard way, so that you have to re read what I say and think about it, so you discover the truths within. As always you can only fully understand and discover all the truths when you put what you have learnt into action. Although the information below is meant to be used in conjunction with your standard therapy in order to speed up the process, some people, I'm sure, could see how the knowledge could be used on the phone to convince a potential client to come and see you instead of a different style of Complementary or Alternative Therapist. Of course, you show them the way to treat themselves for free with the other methods, but suggest to them it will be even better for them if they had a session or two with you.

EXPERIENCE IS THE BEST TEACHER IN LIFE

OBSERVATION AND EXPANSION OF KNOWLEDGE IS THE SECOND BEST

ALWAYS LEARN FROM OTHER'S MISTAKES SO YOU DON'T MAKE THEM

SPIRITUAL DEVELOPMENT IS PURE INTELLIGENCE

WE TREAT FROM THE EYES UP AND DOCTORS TREAT FROM THE EYES DOWN

OVER 90% OF ALL REPORTED ILLNESS IS PSYCHOSOMATIC

OF THE 10% THAT ISN'T, MOST CAN BE HELPED WITH HYPNOSIS

PROBABLY ALL UNREPORTED ILLNESSES ARE PSYCHOSOMATIC

THE HUMAN MIND IS BY FAR THE MOST POWERFUL COMPUTER EVER CREATED

JUST LIKE A COMPUTER, THE PROGRAMMES IN IT CAN BE CHANGED

AROMATHERAPY

The shortcut to aromatherapy is to surround yourself with fresh flowers of the season, the smell (aroma) will naturally get into the air of your house and their bright visible colours will cheer you up. Also surround yourself with plants, by doing this you are returning your body to nature and as such, it will feel better. Also as plants take in the carbon dioxide which we breathe out and in turn give out fresh oxygen, in turn the air in your home will be cleaner and this too will protect your health and make you feel better. Should you wish to actually use the essential oils of the plants, it couldn't be easier, just go to the Body Shop and get the Tisserand leaflet on the oils, this tells you how to use them and what each oil does. The leaflet costs nothing, I recommend the use of the flowers and plants in conjunction with a vaporiser ring and an oil suited to the specific complaint, this is the easiest and I've found, most effective way to use aromatherapy.

REFLEXOLOGY

The shortcut to reflexology is to simply walk around at home barefoot. It is unnatural for our feet to be covered with shoes, which store up a huge electrical charge and as such, knock the body out of balance. If we were to return to nature then we would walk barefoot. Well today it is only safe to do this at home, so do it whenever you are at home and naturally all the points will be stimulated automatically and without effort. The other way, is to massage the whole area of your own or your partners foot and in that way you have got to feel better as a result, as the whole correct point will be massaged.

HERBALISM

As with all the examples I am going to give, return to nature, buy lots of different herbs from the Herbalist and on them it will tell you what food each herb can be added to. If you are adding the herbs to your cooking on a daily basis then it will become unnecessary to use any other form of herbal treatment, as it's natural and automatic. Should you wish to proceed further and make up actual remedies, get a copy of Potters new encyclopaedia of botanical drugs and preparations, with this you can check up which herbs should be used for what problem.

Then the general rules of thumb to follow are as follows: If the herb is on sale to be added to food then it should be safe for use. You give the patient a one month course of treatment for each year they have had the problem. You use one ounce of herb to one pint of boiling hot natural spring water. The contents are placed in a teapot and stirred up and left for about 10 minutes to stand. The liquid is then poured into a strainer and into a bottle for dosage so it's then clear liquid but has the goodness of the herbs within it.

This pint of liquid is to be consumed over the period of one day, so half a pint is drunk the same morning and half a pint that night. It must be used the same day, as no preservative has been added to the mixture, this is called an infusion. If you can't find a strainer, a silk stocking, which has not been dyed, will do the same job if the liquid is poured through it.

Some people add brandy to the mixture so it lasts longer as it acts as a preservative, but I'd advise as above. The other way of preparation is a decoction, this is used with root herbs, such as garlic etc., it's put into a pan with the water and boiled for about the same time as above and then strained, this is the way to get the goodness out of root herbs. By the way, half a pint is basically the amount an average household coffee mug holds, so if you have no jug you could use that as a measure. Lastly, if you use a mixture of 8 herbs, of course one eighth of an ounce of each is used so the total herb total is 1 ounce to 1 pint, then you can't go wrong.

MASSAGE

Regular sex is the best form of massage and relaxation there is, if you do it correctly. Also, by telling your partner what you like and don't it can be fun and beneficial to experiment with your own amateur massage. The art of massage goes back thousands of years and providing you keep to the more gentle strokes, no harm will be done. The golden rule is, JUST FOLLOW YOUR INSTINCTS, but please don't use essential oils in any "sensitive areas".

NATUROPATHY

The basis of this therapy is to return to nature and eliminate any unnatural habits from the patient's life. They may just need more light or more of a kind of food, they may not have a good posture.

By studying your patient and questioning them, common sense will lead you to a correct solution and as in analysis, if you remove the cause of the problem all the symptoms will vanish. For example a friend kept getting corns on her toes, so I knew extra weight must be putting onto her toes. I asked her what she did, any sport? No. Did she have to reach up to high shelves at work? No. Then I asked if she danced. She said she did up until a year or two ago. This explained it. She didn't wear high heels, so I knew that wasn't the cause of the problem. As it turned out, I got her to walk around a bit and without realising it, she was putting more weight onto her toes. I asked what kind of dancing. She said ballroom and then the problem was solved, she had loved ballroom dancing and as it required moving on her toes and her mind had connected this with enjoyment it had become habitual. She then, for a week or two consciously thought of how she was walking and then it became habit not to do this and she has not been troubled with her feet since. So you see it's rather like psycho analysis find the cause of the problem, remove it and the symptoms vanish.

Someone with a bad back usually does office work and no gardening. Nature designed the body to plant things, so if they did some gardening the joints in their body would loosen up. Arthritis is more likely to be usual in people who have used the joints of their body in a repetitive way. (Tai Chi exercises will help stop arthritis.)

HOW TO HELP WITH MEMORY LOSS DISEASES.

If you have any aluminium pans or cooking utensils, throw them away, as, if you keep using them, later in life you are likely to get a mind disease. Aluminium, is highly toxic, but has a coating on it to stop such effects, but once a metal spoon has accidentally scratched this surface off and made the pan or utensil shiny, then the toxic part can get into the food as it's cooked and you then eat the food and as you can see, it's a vicious circle. If you are going to have metal pans and utensils then please have stainless steel. By throwing out items of an aluminium nature of someone with a mind disease already it could help stop the problem getting much worse.

HOW TO HELP WITH LONG AND SHORT SIGHTEDNESS

Both long and short sightedness is in some cases a conditioned problem and as such, a cure of conditioning can be used to help them. If short sighted, these people have probably been used to sitting near the TV and always looked at things close up, or without the correct light etc. If long sighted, then they have probably looked at things from a distance for much of the time. In both cases it has become a conditioned response and by reversing things and conditioning themselves to do the opposite they will very quickly have no need for glasses. Another way to help as well as reversing their habits and acting in a more natural way, is for them to stand outside at night and look at their thumb, (which is near) for a minute and then to look at the sunset (which is far) for a minute and to repeat this at least five times, (takes 10 minutes). Done each day in conjunction with the reversal of their wrong habits, their vision will rapidly improve.

HOW MIRACLES ARE WORKED

There are no miracles and yet there seems to be in the bible and in everyday life, well, I think they omit some of the facts. For example, "he caught loads of fish in a short time", well most people don't know that fish get hungry at sunset so you're more likely to catch them then. A man stands in a field, he utters a strange command and suddenly about 100 birds land at his feet, coming from nowhere. Well, you are stunned, what you didn't see were the three months of effort that went into making this possible. Each day for the past three months at the same time in the same place, rain or shine, that man has gone with three loaves of bread and fed the birds. This time he takes no food, but they see him, it's the right time of day and so they assume food is on the way and all fly down to his feet leaving you to think it was a miracle. Well as I see it, here the real miracle was the effort put in here to engineer the effect. Some psychics say it would be possible to walk on water, but would take 20 years of study, I say why waste 20 years when the next boat will take you across in 10 minutes time.

Women seem to have periods at different times. This is because artificial lighting has had an unnatural effect on their bodies. If you take these women and put them in prison where they are all subjected to the same conditions and lighting etc., then within a short time they will all commence together, at the same time, as that is how nature intended it.

So I hope you now see the secret behind miracles is TIMING, PREPERATION and the creation of a NATURAL environment.

I hope you realise this section has been included in order to make you think and as a result hopefully open your eyes up to nature more and start to realise what has been under your nose all the time.

If the body was conditioned to the climate it's in, as nature intended, then like a friend I have, you'd never need the heating on, would have more money and would never get the common cold or other ailments. Heating etc. is unnatural and man made, so it has to be man broken.

For back pain, sleeping on the floor each night will solve the problem quickly.

WE ARE NOTHING ON THIS EARTH

YES, WE ARE NOTHING, NO PHYSICAL THING

WE ARE NOT A PHYSICAL THING, SO WE MUST BE INTELLIGENCE

THIS MEANS THE INTELLIGENCE RULES THE BODY AND

NOT VICE VERSA

AND ONCE YOU REALISE THAT, well my dear friend when asked who are you? The best reply would be Pure Intelligence. For that is what you are, so it's wise to expand your intelligence all the time and then your quality of life will improve and once you have faith in knowing who you are, everyday illness will be a thing of the past and will not bother you. Until you have faith in that you are stuck in Hell because we create our own Heaven or Hell.

Spiritual yogis take years in temples to find themselves and then are only allowed to leave when they know and have faith in the fact they are nothing. You are pure intelligence and once you know that and realise that is too valuable to destroy, then you will know you are immortal. You will know you will live again and as such, have lived many times before. Knowing this, all worries will leave you; you have all the time in the world and if you don't complete your tasks in this life don't be surprised if you do next time.

You'll also find the things you're really good at now are probably what you did in a previous life and that would explain how you can have child prodigies etc. The body is just a shell and you will get another shell when you leave this one.

Anyway that's the end of this section, I hope it has given you some food for real deep thought, for within it really are many keys which can be used to unlock the doors which may be blocking your success in life.

So observe and expand your knowledge. Know you will be a success and you will be. Again, as the bible says, "As a man thinketh so a man becomes." So I hope you now realise you really are in charge of your own life and that luck is engineered by you.

INCREASING YOUR HYPNOTHERAPY BUSINESS AND INCOME

Below are some keys to increasing your clients and as such, your income. An easy way to get more work is through TV, radio and press publicity and best of all, these can be got for free. To do so, come up with a gimmick, like a novel headline saying The TRANCE of a lifetime, for hypnotist Jonathan or whatever. The headline must be catchy and preferably humorous. This increases your chances of the story getting into print. The press release should be typed in double space format on to single sheets of white A4 paper. You stand a better chance of getting the story in print if you supply a few matt finish black and white photos with the story, as papers prefer to print a story if it has a photo with it. This is what helps to sell papers and make them look more interesting. The release should be short and to the point and of public interest if at all possible. Or you can tie the story in with some event that's in the news etc. and ride on its success.

For example, it hits the news that people are dying of cancer and you offer discount treatment to local people who have cancer and to stop people smoking, as the story is in the news it's topical and up to date and as such, will get in print. This will get you a large, free write up with a photo and on the advert will be the number at which you can be contacted. This will get you many, many clients. I had a write up on noesitherapy in a local paper and offered "free sessions" the article got me 107 enquiries within 24 hours of the paper coming out and of them I converted 87 into clients who paid me, YES, they paid me and it was legal. When they called I explained that they would need about four sessions and half would be free. But so they had to make a commitment they paid for the first two sessions at £25 each and got the second two free. After that there would be a discounted rate of £15 per session. As I say, 87 of the 107 who called were delighted with the offer and it not only earned me much money, but gave me loads of experience within a short space of time. If I really had given the treatment totally for free and not just partly for free then all of them would have come. To do that near national no smoking day, say to the local paper if they pay you a fee they can then offer readers free sessions of smoking cessation therapy and this will help their papers and get them much goodwill and new readers. They then pay you £100 per day for 8 hours of your time (treating 32 clients within that eight hours by doing them in groups of four). The reason for doing it so cheap, is that each person will buy a tape off you at £6.95 to continue the therapy and some may come back again for a paid session. But most important the paper will run two stories, one prior to the event and one after, both giving details of how to contact you and as such, you get loads of clients, plus the "free" clients become walking adverts. Any stunt of this kind should be included in the FREE local paper as more homes will get this and more people see it. When you've done a few things for the paper and got on good terms with them, then it will get to the point where they call you and ask for a story as they are running short of news that week. Each week after such an article you should have a classified wordage advertisement in the paper, giving brief details of your service and contact number. I find I get best results when this goes under the personal column, as more people read this than do the health column. These adverts should appear each week and that way your name stays on their mind and they will come to you first

To get on radio tell them the TV company have shown an interest and they should get in first. To get on TV, tell them a bigger TV production group has shown an interest and they should get in first. It's a competitive business and this trickery will work many more times than you'd think.

My classified produces at least 20 calls a week. Why? And, oh yes, about 18 of them will become paid clients. The advert below is what I include and you would do the same with your own name and number. When they call I explain as above, that one or two sessions are free, this way you are not breaking any laws and they become clients. Isn't business a lot easier than you thought? Being qualified in marketing, finance and management and having been in show business 20 years plus, I know all the tricks and pass them on to others.

The advert I used was worded as follows, with the underlined words being printed in bold print. By the way, FREE, is the most powerful and effective word that you can ever use in an advertisement.

<u>FREE HYPNOTHERAPY,</u> Psycho Analysis, Psychotherapy and Past Life Regression, available from professional of many years experience call, Heywood Hypnotherapy Centre, on XXXX XXXXXX and ask for Jonathan.

The above advert cost me about £10 a week to run in the busiest local paper on the busiest day of the week and it worked wonders. I found that I also got extra business and more word of mouth advertising by offering a small discount in fees to students, unemployed and pensioners.

You don't have to advertise of course, but done properly, it is a very good investment and with every one of your clients being a potential source of further business it makes good sense.

There are many other ways of getting yourself known than the ones I have explained so far and a good pointer is to look at your "opposition". Do regard other therapists in your area as opposition. Each client that your opposition treats is a blow to your business.

Look in your copy of Yellow Pages under hypnotherapists and assess how your own advertisement would look against the others. Yellow pages can be a little expensive compared to other publications, but it does come up with the results. People tend to look here first when seeking therapy of any kind. An advertisement in Yellow Pages also gives you a professional perception. People see it as carrying bonafide advertisers (although this is not strictly true).

If you decide to choose Yellow Pages, you will notice that they cover many different sizes. If you can stretch to it, you will do much better with a quarter column including your own photograph, or at least some type of picture. People warm and respond much better to a human face in an advertisement, especially so with therapy. In this publication, you also get over the principal of having to be visible time after time, before someone responds.

If you are in a rural area, the local church or village magazine can give good results for very little outlay. As an extension to actual therapy, with what you have learned in this course, you have more than enough information to give talks, lectures and seminars to countless numbers of groups and organisations. Start with the local women's institute and prepare yourself for lots of bookings and enquiries.

Small cards in local shops are inexpensive and although do not give high numbers, they do help to get your name established. Strangely enough, dependant on his or her views, your own and surrounding Doctors centres may see you as an asset. Especially if you write a professional letter explaining that you can provide private counselling and psychotherapy.

The last piece of advice in this section will leave your mind racing and your body reaching for a pen to write down all the other potentials which will be stimulated. Design a poster or write out a card carrying your speciality subject as CURING FLYING PHOBIA'S. Pop down to your local travel agent and they will almost pay you to display it!!!!!

Well you now have all the keys you need for success, so now go and use them to open up the doors of opportunity.

PART TWELVE

HOW TO EARN MONEY FROM STRESS MANAGEMENT AND MOTIVATIONAL TRAINING.

It is estimated that in the UK at least 40 million working days are lost each year due to the effects of stress. It is hardly surprising therefore, that practically everyone has heard of stress management training. It has become so common that the majority of middle to large size companies have at some time arranged stress management training for their employees, whilst most colleges run part time stress management classes.

Anyone who is a good communicator and able to manage their own stress responses can capitalise on the growing market for good quality stress management training. It is remarkably easy to obtain lucrative contracts to deliver stress management training, in both industrial and academic environments.

Contrary to most people's belief, no qualifications are required to teach adults, either in the work place or at colleges and other adult education centres. In fact, most part time and adult evening class tutors have absolutely no teaching qualifications. Furthermore, in subjects like stress management, which are non skills specific, it is somewhat of a rarity to find tutors or trainers who hold qualifications in the subject itself.

Instead of qualifications, certain personal qualities are needed to become successful in stress management training. Primarily, these are:

1. Communication skills – the ability to organise your thoughts and ideas in a logical way and to present them clearly and concisely to others, whilst stimulating their appetite for further learning.

2. A belief in the power of the mind to produce physiological effects in the body. A basic understanding of the relationship between mind and body.
3. The ability to get on well with people and to relate to both individuals and groups in a totally non-judgemental way.
4. Patience, understanding and tolerance.
5. The ability to generally control and manage one's own responses to stress provoking situations.

If you feel reasonably confident that you possess each of these qualities and are capable of reading and learning from the wealth of material which exist concerning stress and stress management related topics, there is absolutely no reason why you would not be able to earn a very good income from providing stress management training.

Once you become a regular adult tutor at a college or other adult education centre, you will be offered the opportunity to undertake some part time training, which if successfully completed, provides you with a qualification. An example of such a course and qualification is the City and Guilds Further and Adult Education Teaching Certificate, (F.A.E.T.C.). Whilst stressing again that a qualification is NOT necessary in order for you to teach adults, the F.A.E.T.C. is a very desirable and useful qualification to obtain and the course will provide all that you need to know to become a first class adult education tutor.

Whilst qualifications and actual training experience are not essential, it helps if your background includes some supervision, management, sales or interviewing experience. Any experience which involved working with groups of people such as chairing meetings, youth work, community work or entertainments management would also be extremely useful. Once again though, none of these backgrounds is essential and there are many, very successful stress management trainers who have no relevant background.

Perhaps the easiest way to prove this point, is to describe what stress management consists of. When you have read through the typical course overview which commences in the next paragraph, you will fully appreciate that what is involved could easily be taught by any good communicator, regardless of their background and experience.

Stress Management Course Overview

1. The nature and causes of stress.
    The "fight or flight" response.
    The Physiology of stress.
2. Stress response choices.
3. Sources of stress – personality, lifestyle, environmental and chemical

4. Recognising stress symptoms.
5. The nature and power of the unconscious mind.
6. Relaxation techniques.
7. Self Hypnosis.
8. Goal setting.
9. The role of diet and exercise in stress control

A course programme composed of the above topics would appeal to both adult education centres and employers alike. Before describing some very effective techniques and strategies for marketing and presenting such a course to employers and colleges, I will explain each of the topics in more detail. At the end of this part, I provide you with information about where to obtain sufficient knowledge of your subject so that you can teach it to other people.

The Nature and Causes of Stress

To understand what causes stress and what is happening to us when we experience the symptoms of stress, we need to take a look at the original purpose of stress responses in primitive man.

Flight or Fight Response

In primitive times, a constant stream of life threatening dangers presented themselves and two responses were vitally important for survival. These were the response of flight and the response of fight. Hunting ferocious beasts one day and taking part in a bloody tribal battle the next, primitive man had to respond in either of these two ways if he was going to survive. Running for his life to escape an aggressor who was stronger, or fighting to overcome a lesser opponent. The choice was a simple one and totally appropriate to those times.

Nowadays neither response is appropriate to most of challenges we face in everyday life. Instead, civilisation has brought with it many new and highly complex demands to replace most of the truly life threatening ones.

Everyday we are faced with some sort of challenge – "out of the ordinary demands", if you like. Because our autonomic system cannot differentiate between the various sources of arousal, being stuck in a 20th century traffic jam can produce exactly the same bodily responses as being chased by a woolly mammoth or sabre tooth tiger would have done in our ancestors.

In other words, our primitive response mechanism still works in exactly the same way as it has always done whilst the responses themselves have become less and less appropriate. Fighting your employer when he refuses to promote you is probably going to get you into more trouble than running away from him, but neither response is suitable or sensible. If we cannot respond to challenges in the way we were designed or programmed to do, some conflict is bound to result.

A definition of stress is: The state of arousal with which the body responds to out of the ordinary demands. Or challenges which are imposed upon us.

The Physiology of Stress

The process is an extremely prompt, speedy and efficient one which starts the instant we perceive the challenge. Note the word perceive, because it doesn't have to be a "real" challenge – merely a perceived one.   The challenge, or out of the ordinary demand, sets off a chain reaction of bodily processes which produce an upsurge in strength and energy, the two things we need for the flight or fight responses, of course. But that same surge of energy has no outlet when the chains of civilisation restrain us from fleeing or fighting and as a result we are filled with the all too familiar sensations of frustration and pent up anxiety. We find ourselves unable to run and unable to fight, yet at the same time having to deal with the very same chemical reactions that gave our ancestors the strength to fight and the energy to take flight.

We only need to IMAGINE an out of the ordinary demand to place our system on "stress alert." Some inner impatience, anger or anxiety is enough to produce the same chain reaction of body chemistry. This makes it perfectly possible to create a vicious circle of producing stress from – AN ANXIETY ABOUT STRESS.

Stress Response Choices

We do however have some other choices which are appropriate to 20th century living. We have several in fact, but some are unhealthy choices which in the long term cause far more problems than they solve. Examples of unhealthy choices are smoking, alcohol abuse, over eating, drug misuse etc.

Examples of healthy choices are, relaxation and exercise, because with these we are disconnecting and recharging our systems instead of allowing the energy to build up and overload the system. We must either use up the energy or turn it off.

In fact the whole art of stress management is about learning how to control our responses to stress. We cannot remove stress or remove ourselves from all the sources of stress. But stress only becomes harmful when it is uncontrolled, so learning how to control or manage stress is all that we need to concern ourselves with anyway.

The recognition of this fact is the first step towards reducing the harmful effects of stress in your life.

Sources of Stress

The second step is to recognise the various sources of stress. They can be divided into four main groups:

1.   Personality
2.   Lifestyle

3.   Environmental
4.   Chemical

The personality factors are those which arise from our values, beliefs and behaviour patterns. Your value system is the deepest level of your personality, and from them beliefs are formed which in turn produce behaviour patterns. Trying to alter behaviour without understanding or changing your values and beliefs is doomed to failure.

Real change comes from making changes at the deeper levels of your personality. For example low self esteem is formed from certain values and beliefs we hold about ourselves and our world and low self esteem produces stress. To tackle this source of stress we need to learn more about the underlying values and belief which are producing the loss of self esteem and where appropriate, reconstruct them. Stress management explores various techniques for doing this.

Lifestyle as a source of stress concerns the stressful events which are provoked by the way we live. Research by two American doctors, Holme and Rahe, produced a scale of life events, which were valued according to the amount of adjustment needed to cope with them.

Death of a spouse or child came out top, followed by divorce, separation and imprisonment. At the other end of the scale, the two doctors listed changes in eating habits, taking a vacation and even Christmas.

Environmental sources of stress are things like inadequate housing, unpleasant or unhealthy working conditions, crowded public transport and that sort of thing. What is not quite so obvious and easy to recognise about some of them is that we sometimes pretend to actually enjoy them.

For example, some commuters get a buzz out of the mad rush and the crowded trains. It becomes a way of life to boast about, giving a sense of pride at ones ability to "take it" and cope with it all. Underneath this superficial level of enjoyment, the stress factors are still operating and taking their toll. The person who recognises them and learns to manage the stress responses will be OK, but the person who goes on ignoring them, pretending they do not exist, is undoubtedly heading for trouble.

Chemical sources of stress are substances which act upon our central nervous system to produce the symptoms of stress and anxiety. Many such substances are harmless or even beneficial when taken in relatively small doses.

Examples are:

Caffeine: which is in coffee, coca cola and in tea, is a stimulant which boosts the output of stress hormones. Initially it will make you more alert but later, especially when consumed in large quantities, it will produce symptoms of irritability and cause sleeplessness.

Salt: which increases nervous tension.

Sugar: too much sugar can decrease blood sugar, causing fatigue and irritability.

Nicotine: far from being the relaxing drug smokers often claim it to be, nicotine is actually a stimulant which stimulates the adrenal glands, causing full stress response.

Alcohol: which is a depressant when taken in excess, although it relaxes when drunk in moderation.

Recognising Stress Symptoms

Becoming aware of your own stress responses is not quite as it sounds. Stress distorts perception. We do not notice what is happening as we keep driving ourselves harder. The more stressed we are, the less chance we have of noticing it.

Psychologists sometimes talk about different personality types in relation to stress response. One type is very ambitious, competitive, hard working, impatient and aggressive, actually thrive on stress, getting a "high" from a stress hormone known as noradrenalin. Such a personality can become hooked on this substance and they seem to produce it in greater quantities than other personality types.

Another type of person, often labelled "the over achiever" is equally at risk. This type of person gives the impression of always calmly coping with everything life throws at them. Being tough, proud of being able to withstand the pressure. They will deny the dangers of stress and disapprove of others who "give in", considering that to be a sign of weakness. They are generally unable to admit to any personal limitations of vulnerability.

In reality, pure examples of these character types are rare, most people combining and exhibiting the different qualities according to changing circumstances. Nevertheless, the beliefs that, "stress is something which doesn't affect me" or "something I just have to grin and bear", illustrated by both of these personality types, are extremely widespread.

Stress Symptoms

These can be physical, psychological, or behavioural. Here are some common <u>physical</u> stress symptoms: Chronic stomach upsets, ulcers, bowel disorders, blood pressure, skin rashes, irregular breathing, impotency, insomnia, fatigue, irritable bowel syndrome.

Some examples of <u>psychological</u> symptoms are: Irritability, impatience, restlessness, frustration, hostility, anger, loss of control, apathy, boredom, guilt, shame, helplessness, hopelessness, depression, mood swings.

Examples of <u>behavioural</u> symptoms are: Leaving important things undone, panicking, allowing insufficient time to get to work or to appointments, talking too fast, arguing for the sake of arguing, losing your sense of humour, over reacting with emotional outbursts, suspicions, difficulty with decision making, memory loss, inability to concentrate, loss of discriminatory power, poor judgement, erratic or uncharacteristic behaviour.

<u>The Unconscious Mind</u>

The unconscious is so much wiser and more powerful than the conscious mind. And so it should be, because it holds all of our past experiences, all of our fantasies and all of our future possibilities. All of the things we might recognise are there as well as the things we are capable of having, as well as those we have already thought.

The power of the unconscious mind can work, both for us and against us. The unconscious cannot differentiate between what is real and what is believes is real. An example, which proves this to be the case, occurred in 1964, when a man was found dead in a refrigeration unit. He had become trapped and his body revealed all the correct signs consistent with someone who had frozen to death. That's what you'd expect after being locked inside a refrigeration unit, isn't it?

It's certainly what that man expected and it's exactly what he told his unconscious mind to believe, because if he hadn't he would have lived. The refrigeration unit wasn't switched on and the <u>temperature inside was well above freezing point.</u>

Such is the power of the unconscious mind to work in a negative fashion, but what of its power to work for us? In the USA, research is currently going on to establish exactly how it is, that a significant proportion of terminally ill people are still alive several years after they should have died. The diagnosis for these patients, their circumstances and condition was identical to patients who died within six months of the diagnosis, yet seven or more years later they are still living. The research is still incomplete, but enough is already know to tell us that these patients are using the power of their unconscious mind to create a life giving belief system to overcome the physical effects of their illness.

So, if the power of your unconscious mind is on the one hand capable of killing you and on the other hand, capable of saving you from certain death situations, it is obviously a good idea to harness its power for your well being. What that really means, is learning to make it create positive thoughts and thereby produce positive energy for you.

Relaxation Techniques

Relaxation is just about the most natural thing that anyone could experience. It is also an experience which by definition requires the absence of any effort. Because of its essentially natural and effortless nature, it seems almost paradoxical to suggest that relaxation is a skill that can be acquired and developed through regular practice.

Practicing the art of relaxation in order to become more proficient at it, is however no more paradoxical than practicing any other art or skill. You should be prepared to practice at least twice a week.

To start with, you probably only need five to ten minutes per session. But when you have successfully completed the preliminary exercises, the second stage sessions will require you to devote something like twenty minutes per session.

This is what you do. Simply lie back on whatever you have decided to relax upon, ensure that you are completely comfortable. Allow your eyes to focus on some spot just above your forehead and simply let your mind and body slow down. Do not try to make anything happen or do anything other than allow yourself to rest comfortably with your arms lying loose by your sides and your hands open. If your eyes begin to feel tired or watery, just let them close, but if they are more comfortable remaining open, then allow them to do so.

Your only objective at this stage is to let your mind and body slow down and that will occur automatically, without you trying to make it happen. You'll probably start to notice sensations of tiredness of which you were not previously conscious. Explore these feelings and begin to experience where they are situated. Feel the sensations in the various muscle groups of the arms, legs, neck, shoulders, back and stomach.

After a little while of allowing yourself to experience the sensations in this fairly general way, start to focus your attention on one area of your body at a time. Start with one of your hands. Focus your attention on this hand and concentrate on whatever sensations you can sense there for about ten seconds. Then shift your attention to the other hand and do the same. Next, carry out the same observation of the sensations in your feet, spending about ten seconds on one foot before shifting your attention to the other. After this transfer your attention to gain a similar awareness of the sensations in the various sets of muscles of your face. Consider the ones in your cheeks and the tiny ones surrounding your eyes. Continue by shifting your attention to the muscles of your jaw and the ones surrounding your mouth. Whilst you concentrate on each of these sets of muscles, let them remain as still as possible.

By focusing your attention on specific areas in this way, you will find that the remaining areas of your body lose their tension automatically, whilst your mind learns how to forget that they even exist at all. Repeat the cycle of hands, feet and facial muscles, three more times, dealing with any lapses of concentration in the gentle, detached way I have already described. You have all the time in the world and learning to be really patient with yourself is an essential part of the skill which you are developing.

You will begin to notice how tension that was present when you first started the cycle of awareness of each area melts away with each successive round. The sensations, which were present when you commenced the exercise, are replaced with other sensations and you will become more adept at tuning yourself into the subtle variations with repeated sessions.

Follow the same procedure in subsequent sessions but extend the cycle of areas on which to focus your attention to include the upper arms, the thighs, the calves, the shoulders, the neck and the abdominal region. Eventually, the restlessness and mind wandering which was a feature of your initial attempts will start to disappear and a greater feeling of comfort will be experienced in all areas of your body.

An indication of how near you have come to achieving the objectives of the first stage, preliminary exercises is the degree to which you have now developed the ability to distinguish between the very different and distinct characteristic sensations of tension and relaxation. Further evidence of your progress is the way in which you are now able to direct attention and focus concentration of awareness on any part of your body, whilst all the remaining parts feel as though they have ceased to exist.

Whereas five to ten minutes was all that was required for the first stage exercises, you will probably need about twenty minutes for each session of the stage exercises. Proceed exactly as you did for the preliminary exercises, but now you are actually going to deliberately induce tension into various areas of your body.

Start with one of your arms. With the rest of your body relaxed, focus your attention on the arm and slowly raise it about six inches above its resting position. Introduce a little more tension into the arm, concentrating your entire awareness on how it feels as you allow it to stiffen and become very straight. Explore the sensations in your fingers and follow them through the rest of your hand, up your forearm, through your elbow and into your upper arm. Switch attention to your other arm and repeat the process.

When you have been right through the process with each arm and fully recognised the subtleties of the varying sensations of tension and relaxation in each, go right through the whole exercise again, but this time without raising your arms. Instead of using the physical process of raising, stiffening and straightening your arms to induce tension, induce the tension and letting go by mentally giving yourself suggestions. Keeping the suggestions at the level of unspoken thoughts, silently say to yourself: "My muscles are tensing. They are becoming more and more tense." Repeat this suggestion a number of times whilst focusing your attention on the arm which is being tensed.

When you are ready to move into the relaxation phase, say something like: "Let go – my arm is relaxing now." Followed by: "I'm letting go completely." And: "All of the tension is melting away." Repeat these suggestions as you continue to focus your attention upon the resting arm letting go of its tension and becoming more and more relaxed.

Induce and relieve tension in the legs in exactly the same way. Physically at first, then mentally, by silently issuing suitable suggestions. After you have completed the leg muscle exercises, explore the sensations of tension and the absence of tension in the small of your back. This is carried out physically by slightly arching your back, holding the muscles tense, then drawing in the stomach muscles.

Finally, produce and relieve the tension mentally, using similar suggestions to those used during the previous exercises. Go through the same procedure with the muscles of your face, head, and neck. Focus all of your attention on the experiences and feelings you receive. Carried out properly, these relaxation exercises will produce some extremely pleasant, almost euphoric moments of mental detachment during the periods of rest.

Self Hypnosis

Self hypnosis is a completely safe, natural, everyday phenomena, experienced by all of us in one way or another. It may be accurately defined as: "A state of relaxation and concentration at one with a state of heightened awareness, induced by suggestion."

There is no special skill or knowledge needed to practise self hypnosis. It is merely a natural extension of the relaxation techniques, described earlier. Having become deeply relaxed, counting down from five to zero and focusing on the idea of each count being a step deeper into relaxation and calm, is all that is required to achieve the state we call hypnosis.

From that point on, self hypnosis is all about giving yourself positive suggestions aimed at the subconscious mind. Because you are using self hypnosis to help manage stress the suggestions will be about stress coping skills. For example: "I feel calm and assertive when I am criticised at work". There are many books available about self hypnosis and the power of auto suggestions. The distance learning package, "Positive Changes", is particularly recommended.

Setting Goals

Stress occurs when we feel that events control us, instead of us being in control of events. Having clearly defined goals helps to create a sense of being in control. Changes cannot occur, successes cannot be achieved, habits cannot be overcome and improvements cannot be made, unless goals are specifically and clearly defined at the outset.

The best way to set goals is to sit down with a pen and some paper and brainstorm for as long as it takes you to come up with some really clear and totally compelling goals. The best goals are those which are not only specific but are also inspirational.

Having listed in precise details, the goals you wish to set yourself, you will next need to draw up a blueprint which plans the route between where your now and where you will be when you achieve your goals. The way to do this is to start with the ultimate long term goals and to break down into ever increasing detail, describing the various stages of action that will have to be accomplished on route if you are to reach your final destination. This process will involve quantifying things, making each outcome measurable and allocating specific periods of time for the completion of each stage.

It is also essential that the targets you set yourself are realistic and obtainable. The achievement of one small step towards a goal has a snow balling effect which makes each of the subsequent steps become easier and easier as you progress. Making that step a little too steep can have the opposite effect, causing a negative spiral of mini failures and deflated ego to develop. This prevents the ultimate goals from ever being achieved.

The way to ensure that you really do attain your goals is to regularly rehearse achieving them. You can actually rehearse attaining goals with the help of self hypnosis. Visualise yourself carrying out your plan and accomplishing the things you have set out to accomplish.

The Relationship Between Stress and Diet

The relationship between stress diet has been affected by the developments of our sophisticated lifestyle. In primitive man, an automatic balance of energy input and energy output was sustained for most of a man's life. He burnt the right amount of calories to fuel his body for warmth and physical exertion. Today, it is not like that. Physical work is becoming the exception rather than the norm and even for those of us who are still engaged for most of our time in physically demanding work, the nature of the tasks we perform are quite unlike the exertions of our hunter, gatherer ancestor.

On the other side of the equation, foods, especially rich, fattening ones, are plentiful. Twentieth century man can no longer expect nature to provide an automatic balance between diet and exercise. It's up to us to take the appropriate action to introduce the balance ourselves.

It's easy enough to find out what to do. There's a multi-million pound industry of diet plans, exercise programmes, books, tapes and video information on the subject. There are many good diet plans, but whatever one you choose, make sure that it includes fresh fruit, vegetables and fibre.

The other thing to ensure is that you eat regularly and peacefully. Stop for meals. Put away your work. Relax. Put that book down. Don't answer the telephone. Just sit down and really relax to savour every mouthful of whatever it is you choose to eat.

Stress and Exercise

Motivate yourself to start taking enjoyable, regular exercise. Exercise has an immediate effect on anxiety. It is also an ideal outlet for tension, bottled up aggression or frustrations.

Other benefits are:

Improved sleep
Fewer stress related aches and pains
Greater inner calm
Improved mental clarity
Better powers of concentration

Exercise releases brain chemicals:

Endorphins = happiness and euphoria – thereby dispelling anxiety and depression.

There are basically six types of exercise to choose from. Deciding which ones to include in your personal exercise programme is a case of checking out which types satisfy your specific needs. The exercise you choose has to be enjoyable, forcing yourself to do exercises you don't enjoy is going to be a pretty stressful thing to do.

Types of Exercise

Aerobic dance

Requires approximately 2 hours a week
Increases flexibility of movement
Strengthens abdominal and leg muscles
Excellent for cardiovascular endurance

Aerobic exercise

Can be jogging, hill walking, cycling or swimming

Requires 10 – 15 minutes daily
Promotes flexibility if preceded by simple warm up exercise
Strengthens leg muscles. Swimming also increases upper body strength
Second to none for strengthening heart and lungs and improving overall
stamina.

Calisthenics

Requires 30 minutes daily
Stretching exercises particularly useful for improving all over flexibility.
Can improve cardiovascular endurance but best results achieved when
supplemented by aerobic exercise

1. Yoga
Requires 30 minutes per day and a regular class
Excellent stress reliever and muscle tension relaxer
Improves flexibility in all parts of the body
Offers only minimal cardiovascular improvement

2. Weight Training
Requires approximately 30 minutes, three times weekly, in a suitably
equipped fitness club
Excellent for strength building
Improves flexibility if correctly executed
Offers only minimal cardiovascular improvement

3. Martial Arts
Requires twice weekly attendance at 1 – 2 hour class
Stretching exercises and high kicks are excellent for improving flexibility.
Push ups and sit ups are usually a main part of training and these help to
build strength.
Cardiovascular endurance is improved considerably through most martial
arts, with the possible exception of Tai Chi.

Other Stress Management Topics

Here is an alternative list of stress management training topics for you to
consider. Perhaps you will need to read up on a few more of the topics but
there is a wealth of information available about all of them:

Managing Change:

Relationship between Stress and Change
Accepting Personal Responsibility for Change
Identifying aspects of behaviour which can be modified to accommodate change.
Making our responses to changing circumstances a positive experience.
Time Management
Compiling and Using Positive Affirmations
Creative Visualisation

How to make a Proposal to Colleges

When approaching a college or adult education centre, you will need to submit a proposal in a form which shows that you are organised and have carefully planned the design and delivery of your training. Here is an example.

Stress Management Course Overall Course Objectives

To enable students to examine and understand the causes and effects of stress.
To provide them with techniques and strategies for reducing the levels of stress in their lives and for effectively managing responses to potentially stressful situations.
To demonstrate the power that is contained in every person's mind and to teach students how to tap this inner resource and utilise its positive energy.

Day One – Two Hours

Session 1: Introductions. Overview and aims of course.

Objectives:
To "break the ice" and help students to feel relaxed in group setting
To ensure course content matches students' expectations and if not, to resolve any misunderstandings etc.

Session 2: "What is Stress?"

Objectives
To offer a definition of stress
To enable students to understand the physiology of stress
To enable students to understand the "fight or flight" response.
To examine the sources of stress, personality, lifestyle, environmental and chemical.

Session 3: "How stressed are you? Part one"

Objectives
To complete a "self assessment" exercise

Day Two – Two Hours

Session 1: "How stressed are you? Part two"

Objectives
To help students recognise their stress responses
To understand stress symptoms and signals
Review of self assessment exercise

Session 2: The Unconscious Mind

Objectives
To enable students to understand the nature and power of the unconscious mind
To show that this power can be controlled for positive benefits or can be left uncontrolled to work negatively on occasion.

Day Three – Two Hours

Session 1: Relaxation

Objectives
Students will learn and practice the techniques of deep relaxation

Day Four – Two Hours

Session 1: What is Self Hypnosis?

Objectives:
To reveal the nature of hypnosis
To establish its value as a practical tool with which the unconscious mind can be programmed for beneficial effect.

Day Five – Two Hours

Session 1: Other Stress Management Strategies

Objectives
To provide background material explaining the role of diet and exercise in stress control
To introduce students to the concept of meditation
To briefly describe other popular aids to stress proofing. (e.g. aromatherapy, nutrition and massage.)

Session 2: Course Evaluation

Objectives
To check students understanding of course material
To answer unresolved questions
To help students consider ways of maintaining and further developing strategies to manage stress in the future.

Having prepared a course outline, showing the learning objectives for each session, similar to the example above, you will need to send it with a covering letter to colleges and other adult education providers in your area.

Adult part time courses start mainly in January and September and it is a good idea to time your approach well in advance of these months. Write a letter modelled on the example below and enclose your proposed course outline with it.

Mr.............
Adult Education Tutor
.... Adult Education Centre

Dear Mr …………

I am writing to introduce myself and offer to teach Stress Management at your centre.

I have an extensive knowledge of my subject and believe that I am an effective communicator, in both group and one to one situations. (Mention here any relevant experience or qualifications that you have.)

The enclosed example of a course outline is based upon ……. Hours tuition, spaced over ………weeks. It can however be adapted to fit other lengths of time and I would be delighted to meet with you to discuss how best to tailor the proposal to suit your centre's actual requirements.

I would appreciate it if you could telephone me at the above number when you have had sufficient time to consider the proposal.

Yours sincerely

Fees from Adult Education Work

Colleges are fairly consistent in their payment to adult education tutors who are employed on a sessional basis. At the time of writing, all colleges in my own county pay £14 per hour. A neighbouring county is paying £16. This may not sound like a lot of money if you are doing only one, two hour evening class per week, but there is no reason why you should not be able to teach at different centres four nights per week and possibly do a two hour Saturday morning session as well. Your income from adult education work could therefore total as much as £160 per week.

How to Market Stress Management to Employers

It is unusual to find employers who employ less than one hundred people interested in running stress management courses. Rather than waste your time and resources in approaching these smaller companies therefore, it is better to concentrate on reaching those who employ over 150 employees and who have a heavy concentration of technical, administrative, sales and managerial occupations.

You can discover who these employers are within the geographical area in which you decide to operate, by referring to the detailed records held by the local chamber of commerce or public library.

Initially, it is best to aim for a "mailing list" comprising of fifty to one hundred employers. You will need to research the name of the personnel and training director or manager. If the company does not employ one, obtain the name of managing director or most appropriate decision maker. If this information isn't readily available, a simple telephone enquiry to the company is usually sufficient to ascertain it.

When your initial list is complete, prepare a letter similar to the one set out below.

Dear………. (Training and Personnel Director if Possible)

It is estimated that in the UK at least 40 million working days are lost each year due to the effects of stress. But the cost to industry doesn't end there, because the figure only relates to actual absences from work. Stress produces several other effects. Over-stressed employees at any level of a company are inefficient employees. At clerical and operative level, stress might reveal itself in carelessness, poor timekeeping and absenteeism. Whilst at more senior levels, creativity, judgement and decision making skills are affected.

It would be unrealistic to talk about eliminating stress. On the other hand, learning how to manage stress is something that everybody can do and benefit enormously from, which is why I offer Stress Management Training for people at work.

My training helps people to recognise stress symptoms, discover and understand its root causes, use "good" stress to their advantage and to deal with "bad" stress by adopting appropriate coping skills.

Your employees will come back from their course of Stress Management refreshed, confident and relaxed. But more importantly, permanent effects can be achieved with everyone who follows our simple programme of post course practice. To help to ensure that course participants continue to progress and develop their skills, I like to arrange a follow-up session six months after the course. The increased efficiency of the employees you have selected for training will repay their course fees many times over, whilst the personal benefits which each individual experiences from attending a course promotes a sense of appreciation that they are employed by a caring employer.

I appreciate that you may need to consult with other personnel before deciding whether you would like to meet with me and discuss the details of what the training has to offer your company. With your permission, therefore, I propose to telephone you two weeks from now to enquire whether you have been able to consider the contents of this letter.

Yours sincerely

Another idea is to produce a brochure which describes the training you are offering. This is posted out with a slightly shorter sales letter which draws attention to the contents of the brochure. You would still conclude with your proposal to follow up by a telephone call and in either case, it is important that you do in fact make the call at the time you have specified.

The telephone call would go something like this:

Hello, is that Mr Jones, the Personnel Director?

My name is………. And I wrote to you a couple of weeks ago about stress management training. Do you recall the letter? Having read the material I sent you, when would be a good time for me to meet you and explain exactly what the training consists of and how your company could benefit from it. Would next Thursday be convenient or would you prefer some other day?

How much to Charge

Although you will come across some competition, it is important that you do not try to sell your stress management training on price. Point out to the employer that you are a specialist – A Stress Management Consultant, as opposed to a run of the mill training company who offer training in a wide range of subjects.

If you give the employer the idea that your training is cheap, he will also assume it's not worth having. If you present yourself as a specialist, offering quality training which can be customised to suit the requirements of the particular company, you can actually get away with making it more expensive than your competitors. Do some research of your own first and find out what your competitors are offering and what their fees are. As mentioned earlier, rates in excess of £500 per day are not at all uncommon.

A guideline base figure for you to consider might be in the region of £30 per day per trainee. A group of between ten and fifteen trainees is about the right size for stress management training, so a one day training course, based on this rate, would give you an income of between £300 and £450.

Appendix

Suggested Background Reading and Further Study

Courses Covering Most of the Topics of Stress Management:

Positive Changes Personal Development Distance Learning Course available from:

The Professional Stress Consultants Course.
The Advanced Stress Consultants Course
Both available from:
Associated Stress Consultants
The Old Vicarage
Clawton
Nr Holdsworthy
Devon
EX22 6PS

Professional Hypnotherapy Courses are available from:

The International Association of Hypno-Analysts
P O Box 180
Bournemouth

BH8 8NH

British Hypnosis Research
8 Paston Place
Brighton
BN2 1HA

Teaching Adults

Adult Learning Adult Teaching
An excellent publication available only from:
The Publications Officer
Publications Unit
Department of Adult Education
"C" Block
Cherry Tree Buildings
University Park
Nottingham
NG7 2RD

Books on Stress Management Related Topics

Stress Control Through Self Hypnosis by Dr Arthur Jackson
Awaken the Giant Within by Anthony Robbins
Relax and Live by Dr Jack Gibson
Stress Management for Wellness by W Schafer

All of the above books can be obtained from:

The Anglo American Book Company
Underwood, St Clears
Carmarthen
Dyfed
SA33 4NE
Tel: 01994 230400

No More Fears by Dr Douglas Hunt – Useful information about the nutritional approach to stress management.
Creative Visualisation by Ronald Shone
Stress Busters by Robert Holden
Burnout by Ken Powell
Introducing Neuro-Linguistic Programming by Joseph O'Connor an John Seymour

All of the above books can be obtained from:

Thorsons Mail Order
Harper Collins Publishers Ltd
Westerhill Road
Bishopbriggs
Glasgow
G64 2QT

The Book of Stress Survival by A Kirsta/Publisher: Guild.

Now I'm sure you'll agree the previous pages on "How to make money from stress management training" by myself, a professional therapist, are both highly informative and also contain information which can earn you back the entire cost of this training course many times over.

From my own personal point of view the only things I can add on the subject of stress management training are as follows:

Read all books you can by Anthony Robbins i.e. Unlimited Power, Awaken the Giant Within and also purchase all his audio courses. Do this and not only will you have all the knowledge required to earn from stress management but you'd also be able to run motivational training sessions also, which can also be highly profitable. One other book on stress management which I'd highly recommend is "Stress Management Techniques", subtitled "Managing people for healthy profits" by Dr Vernon Coleman. It's by Mercury Bodis, 44 Hill Street, London W1X 8LB and order number is 1SBN 1 85251 0366.

Don't forget also that not only is the "Positive Changes" distance learning course as detailed in this chapter useful reading material. But it is also a highly profitable business venture in itself which can earn you a high income indeed. For full details contact, Positive Changes as stated earlier in the chapter.

I will now end this chapter with an example sales letter of my own for Stress Management and Motivational Sales Training. Incidentally, as you offer a 100% confidential service, you aren't allowed to tell customers which media stars you've motivated in the past.

STRESS IN THE WORKPLACE?

Ignore this at your peril. Already companies are in court paying out thousands and thousands in compensation for under estimating this serious issue. Individual company reports carried out, also lectures given. Our counselors are qualified with over 20 years experience in this industry.

We use only the most up to date, tried, tested and proven to work techniques to effect positive change in your company's workforce.

40 million working days per year are being lost to employers as a result of stress related absences. Our services will prove that prevention is better than cure and will save your company thousands of pounds in lost manpower and revenue.

Unlike most other personal development training consultants, Jonathan himself is a successful professional hypnotherapist, psychotherapist and psychological counsellor with a vast experience of dealing with Major Blue Chip Companies and Organisations.

Personal support and guidance is provided in response to individual's needs as well as group motivational training and stress management sessions being held to enable your workforce to operate at peak performance consistently.

As one director was heard to say after a Royle training session:
"My job as the boss is to provide the right atmosphere in the "greenhouse" of our company, so that people can constantly grow. Jonathan Royle's training sessions provide that environment."

ABOUT YOUR TUTOR

Now considered to be one of Britains most dynamic personal development consultants, sales advisors and motivational trainers, Jonathan Royle is also an accomplished stress management consultant and shares his experiences and techniques in a highly effective and entertaining down to earth style.

LIFE CHANGES

Now for the first time, you can hear and experience for yourself, his techniques for confident communication and personal improvement in his "Lifechange" seminars.

Lifechanges is a genuine product and a unique service which is of invaluable use to all company managers, self employed people and in fact, every human who wishes to effect positive and lasting change in their lifestyles.

YOU WILL LEARN

"Powerful communication skills for business and winning solutions for life."

SO DON'T FORGET

"Innovative business leaders are measured by results and not by efforts."

And

"People don't plan to fail, but many do fail to plan."

THE SOLUTION

Well as Henry David Thoreau said, "Things do not change, we change." Jonathan Royle's Lifechanges seminars and lectures teach you and your workforce how to take immediate control of your mental, emotional, physical and financial destiny.

Through inspirational anecdotes, case studies personalised self help tests and a program that anyone can follow, Jonathan Royle teaches the lessons in destine that lead to success through self mastery.

The only limitations we have in life, are those which we impose upon our own minds. So take control of your life and allow Alex Leroy to make you a no limits person.

DREAMS DO COME TRUE

"The only way to discover the limits of the possible is to go beyond them into the impossible"

Arthur C Clarke

Lifechanges seminars can program your mind and guarantee you the success you so richly deserve and as Mark Twain so correctly said.

"There is nothing training cannot do, nothing is above its reach, it can turn bad morals to good, it can destroy bad principles and recreate good ones, it can lift men to angelship."

THE LAST WORD

Our courses can be tailored to suit your individual or company needs and have in the past taught self hypnosis, creative visualisation, neuro linguistic programming, subliminal communication and many other highly effective techniques to numerous satisfied customers to achieve self improvement, stress management, business skills, self awareness, personal growth, career development, habit cessation, increased performance and much more.

Whatever your problem is, Lifechanges can solve it for you. Our courses are an exciting voyage of self discovery which guide you across an ocean to a new world of opportunity and success.

To put your company back onto the track of guaranteed success, increased performance from your workforce and ultimately higher profits give me a call today.

HOTLINE NUMBER

(XXXX) XXXXXX

Top television Hypnotist Jonathan Royle has already used his pioneering techniques to help famous media and sporting stars to effect positive change and increased performance in their careers and lifestyles. Major household name blue chip companies, have also benefited enormously from Royle's confidential service. So remember, if you don't contact Lifechanges, then your <u>competitors will.</u>

SUCCESS CAN BE YOURS – RING NOW

Stress costs your company over £1000 per employee per year. So if your company employs 100 people then stress costs the company over £400 per day. If your company employs 1000 people, then stress costs the company over £1,000000 a year. In an average lifetime, the average employee loses one and a half years from work because of stress induced illness. Whatever else you try, and however much you spend on high technology equipment, nothing will improve your company's efficiency and profitability more than taking care of your employees. Reducing their exposure to stress and learning how to get the best out of them. Your company's biggest hidden asset is the people it employs.

In Jonathan Royle's "Lifechanges" seminars, Jonathan explains exactly how, why and when stress causes problems. More importantly, he also explains how you can control and minimise the amount of stress in your company to consequently have staff perform at their peak performance and to increase the profitability of your company.

If you follow the above principals, you will soon be in control of your own Stress Management Consultancy.

<u>**PART THIRTEEN**</u>

**THE FAST PHOBIA CURE TREATMENT KNOWN AS NEURO
ASSOCIATIVE CONDITIONING (NAC)**

Welcome to part eighteen, which will teach you the treatment developed
and pioneered by top American motivationalist Anthony Robbins. His
treatment is known as Neuro Associative Conditioning or N.A.C. for short.
Full details of this treatment can be obtained free of charge by borrowing
Mr Anthony Robbin's book "Awaken the Giant Within", from your local
library. I believe Mr Robbins entitled his treatment N.A.C as it works
rapidly, just as Neuro Linguistic Programming techniques do, but with this
treatment a strong neurological change is effected within the patient's
body by the thoughts instilled into their minds. It is this change in their
neurological behaviour as a result of the original thoughts in their mind,
which makes the treatment so successful.

In this part, I will introduce you to the subject, so that you can put it to
immediate use, in a similar fashion as was demonstrated on Paul
McKenna's Network First programme, which was broadcast on ITV
during Spring 1995. On this 60 minute documentary, we were clearly
shown that after a therapy session of between 30 to 60 minutes maximum,
a female patient, once scared of flying, not only flew in an aeroplane, but
was relaxed and happy whilst doing so. A man once scared of spiders was
happy to let a furry looking tarantula spider walk all over his palms. And a
woman, once scared of heights, successfully completed a bungee jump
from a great height after only one treatment session.

The same week on Central TV's Friday Night late show "Central Weekend

Live", we were treated to a discussion on this treatment method and the network first programme. Live on TV we saw another man, once petrified of spiders, now able to handle a tarantula after just a brief treatment session with the therapist responsible for all these dramatic sounding case studies, Mr Michael Breen, a good friend of Mr Paul McKenna, who made the Network First programme.

The McKenna documentary also showed step by step, how and why the treatment worked, so if you can obtain a copy of the broadcast shown as I say in Spring 1995, then you will be shown with the aid of visual and verbal tuition the basics of how and why this treatment works.

The treatment shown on the McKenna show has a huge similarity with N.A.C., as taught by Anthony Robbins, so read Awaken the Giant Within and you too can achieve such dramatic results as those I've just mentioned. Now you know what is possible with this unique treatment, which I call "The thirty minute fast phobia cure", because it's a fast phobia cure and the one session the patient will require, will take approximately thirty minutes. Sometimes as long as an hour, but usually an average, somewhere in between. In Mr Robbins book, he details how using this N.A.C. treatment, he has also stopped people from smoking, over eating and other bad habits as well as curing fears and phobias. It seems obvious from all I've seen, that this is the treatment of the future, enabling you to solve most patients' problems in the space of just one session of one hours duration (maximum).

Imagine this, if you used noesitherapy for pain control and N.A.C. for fears, phobias and bad habits, then you'd instantly be able to set up in practice and treat most all clients for most all problems in just one session of no more than one hours duration. Earning a fee of £35 to £50 an hour, (minimum) you could treat 40 clients a week on a 9am to 5pm five day basis and that should bring you an income of between £1400 and £2000 per week. That's a possible income of £104,000 per year which by anyone's standards is a good income and as you could treat clients in their own homes you wouldn't even need an office or expensive equipment. So you'd practically be in profit and earning big money from day one.

Now down to a little theory, so that you can then put this treatment into practice. Firstly consult the illustration which is the last page of this chapter. It shows exactly how N.A.C., Neuro Associative Conditioning, (the master system) and the psychology of change works. You will see a diagram of the human mind, showing that the mind bases everything in life on how much pain or pleasure it causes the person to do or not to do that particular thing. So for example, if a person's mind has stored memories which make smoking seem pleasurable, e.g. the person has stored associations between smoking and relaxing etc. and as such, it becomes hard to stop smoking due to the pleasurable, neurological associations the person has made in their mind and body with direct regards to the action of smoking.

So obviously, if enough painful neurological associations were to be programmed into their mind and body with regards to smoking then it will become an automatic reflex action NOT to smoke, as it would be too painful to the person to smoke due to the neurological associations made between the patient's mind and body by N.A.C. treatment. The basic principle behind how the treatment works is the same whatever it is you are intending to treat. So to stop over-eating you'd have to create enough neurological links between the patients mind and body to make it painful for them to overeat and very pleasurable for them not to eat. Whereas their present behavioural patterns show they are associating pain with not eating and pleasurable associations with eating.

So to put it bluntly, it would seem that if a patient wants to stop a habit or stop some form of behaviour which is inappropriate, eg fears and phobias, then neurological associations between their mind and body must be made to make it painful to do this, to carry on the habit or to have that fear or phobia and you must also make it pleasurable not to do these things or to react in these ways. If a patient wishes to be able to do something, achieve something (ie improved sports performance, more energy, more confidence etc.) then you must create a strong painful neurological association between their mind and body not to do these things and strong associations of pleasure to be connected with both doing and achieving these things.

Put another way, the strong pleasurable associations must always be used to achieve the patients goals, hence it says "towards values" on the picture and strong painful associations must always be connected to the behaviour or habits which they do not wish to continue with, hence it the picture it says, states of pain = away values. Knowing this, once the patient has set their goal and for the following example we'll use a fear of spiders. You just need to follow the six master steps to change as shown on the picture and then success will be yours.

SIX MASTER STEPS TO CHANGE

Decide what you really want and what's preventing you from having it now. Eg. You want a relaxed life full of confidence in all you do. But your fear of spiders prevents you from having it now.

Get leverage = Associate massive pain to not changing this behaviour now and massive pleasure to the experience of changing now. E.g. The pain of not changing now would be panic attacks each time you saw a spider. Feelings of inferiority and a lack of confidence etc. Whereas the pleasurable points of changing now are that you'd have no fear of spiders, increased confidence, feelings of great happiness and a sense of great achievement in all that you do. Which of course would be a far more appropriate form of behaviour for you to have.

Interrupt the limiting pattern. E.g. Once in the hypnotic state which will increase the success of this six step process, although it can and often is as successful without the use of hypnosis, you then interrupt the limiting pattern through the use of visualisation. As shown on Paul McKenna's network first broadcast, for a fear of spiders you'd visualise the tarantula spider talking with a squeaky voice, wearing a funny party hat, with welly boots on eight feet and a big red clown's nose. In other words, you change that mental image of a spider from something that scares you to something you find hilarious. In fact, to the point where you physically laugh at the thought that anyone could be scared of this strange and silly image in your mind. At this point the neurological limiting pattern will have been broken and mentally you are not scared of this image you have created.

Create a new, empowering alternative. E.g. Here again through mental visualisation you'd see in your minds eye that each and every time in the future when you see a spider you will instantly bring the stupid and silly mental image you have created to mind. And as such, will feel calm, relaxed, happy and in fact, a little jovial in this, a situation which once bothered you. See yourself in your minds eye feeling proud, happy and confident with your new behaviour and you will then have created a new, empowering alternative.

Condition the new pattern until it's consistent. E.g. Where you'd have several mental rehearsals, where you'd rehearse reacting to the sight of a spider with the comical mental image and calm confident behaviour. So in your minds eye, imagine seeing a spider, then rehearse reacting in your new calm and confident manner, now no longer scared of spiders due to the new neurological associations you will have made.
TEST IT. E.g. Quite simply, what it says, once all the other five steps have been made, pain has been associated with not achieving your goal, pleasure with achieving it and the limiting pattern has been interrupted, you will then be ready to test your new behaviour in a real life situation. In other words, now is when you confront what were once your worst fears to prove 100% to yourself that they are no longer things that bother you. An ideal test would be to allow a tarantula to be placed on your palms, as shown on the Network First show. Once you have it on your palm, allow the comical mental image to resurface, notice how calm and confident you feel. Then the treatment will be complete and your belief and expectancy would be 100% total and your new behavioural patterns will be set for life.

Here, let me say, to have seen a video of a past patient confronting their fears after this N.A.C. treatment would instill extra belief into you prior to the treatment, which would help ensure success in one session only.

SUMMING UP

Follow the six master steps to change, as outlined in this chapter and follow the other rules as outlined in this chapter and success with N.A.C. will be yours. In this chapter you have learnt all you need to know to, with a little common sense, adapt what I have taught you, so that you can treat practically any patient for any fear, phobia, habit or nervous disorder. Further details can be obtained from Mr Robbin's book, Awaken the Giant Within. And of course, I'd recommend you obtain a copy of the McKenna broadcast and even The Hypnotic World of Paul McKenna book, which contains Mr McKenna's own experiences and thoughts on this treatment. Many psychologists take weeks to do what you can now do in less than one hour using N.A.C. treatment. All I need to mention once again is the importance of facing up to your fear as step six of the treatment. So that when you survive it with no ill effects it concrete's the new mental images in your mind and ensures that you never fear that subject matter again.

With the case of habits etc., time is the test here, so here don't light up a cigarette to prove it makes you feel sick. Do, however, dispose of all ashtrays, tobacco, lighters etc., so that no temptations exist for you.

This six step plan correctly followed will ensure success and achieve the patient's goals. Remember also, that they are first placed under hypnosis and this will ensure that the new comical mental images, as in this example, will always spring to mind, when that once fearful event occurs, in order to ensure you are calm and relaxed. You can also, prior to removing them from trance, implant a major post hypnotic suggestion along the lines of that if ever they do feel the slightest bit of fear in such a situation, then by just taking 3 deep breaths in and then out, the patient will instantly feel calm, confident and relaxed. This gives the power of N.A.C. treatment combined with a powerful post hypnotic suggestion and as such, the old behaviours will be out and the new ones in.

I'll end this chapter, by saying this. Treatment alone can change peoples lives for the better and at the same time earn you an income and lifestyle others only dream of.

<u>**PART FOURTEEN**</u>

**MORE SHORTCUTS TO HYPNO AND PSYCHOTHERAPY
OR HOW TO EARN AS YOU LEARN**

A BRIEF EXPLANATION OF THE THERAPIES

A professional and ethical therapist will always discharge each and every client from treatment at the earliest possible moment, consistent with that client's good care and will also offer the client the style of treatment which ultimately will be most beneficial for them and not necessarily the most profitable for you. The reason for this being, not only is it ethical practice, but in this way, you will only end up with happy clients, who will go off and sing your praises to other people and as word of mouth advertising is by far, the most profitable and effective you will ultimately benefit more in this way.

The therapist undertakes to respect a client's confidentiality at all times and would not even disclose to a spouse or parent that they were undergoing treatment. The ethical therapist will also ensure that any hypnotic (or post hypnotic) suggestion given to any client will be so worded, that any effects can only be beneficial to the client. He/she will have a clear understanding of the concept of symptom substitution, (which, without being too technical, means the possibility of switching from say, agoraphobia to claustrophobia) and in consequence, will only use what is popularly termed "suggestion therapy" for the more minor problems, where the probable substitution can be foreseen and thus controlled. (E.g. anti smoking therapy would contain suggestions to avoid over eating.)

In therapeutic circumstances there is no question of being controlled or manipulated or even induced into a deep trance state. A person in hypnosis (often referred to conscious hypnosis) is not "asleep", they are often more aware of what is taking place than usual and their senses function more efficiently than normal. In normal therapeutic circumstances, nobody could be made to do or say anything they would not want to. Everyone (except the truly mentally sub normal, very young boys and inebriates) can enter the hypnotic state. People who say or think, "nobody could get me under" or "I wouldn't want anyone controlling my mind", or "I might blurt my secrets out", are really demonstrating that they have a total misconception of what hypnosis really is. The state of hypnosis, a totally natural phenomenon, is most pleasant and particularly relaxing and a person can converse quite easily whilst within the state. It is inconceivable that any harm could befall them. Indeed the centuries old technique of hypnosis is being used increasingly as an adjunct to orthodox medicine where it is proving a valuable alternative to drugs for anaesthesia, to accelerate healing, relieve stress and control pain.

A good definition of hypnosis is "a state of relaxation and concentration at one with a state of heightened awareness induced by pure verbal suggestion." The therapist uses his or her voice to induce you into the state of hypnosis and although you are unlikely to feel "hypnotised" as such, you will most probably experience a feeling of mental and physical relaxation and your memory may well be enhanced. You will find that the therapist is a caring professional person, totally devoid of any mystical or magical powers. No flowing robes or swinging watches, just a reassuring manner to put you at ease and the expertise to help with you problem. There are two entirely different treatments using conscious hypnosis and these are as follows:

Suggestion Therapy

Which is used for simpler problems, such as smoking, nail biting, pre test nerves, slimming, relaxation, confidence boosting etc., which require one or two sessions, with perhaps a booster session, several months on. Usually the client receives one session of therapy and prior to being awoken is given the major post hypnotic suggestion, that each time they listen to the audio tape you give them it will have just the same effect with them as if you were in the room with them. They are awoken and for the next few days they listen to the tape which strengthens the suggestions in their mind for the type of therapy of habit cessation they've had.

Analytical Therapy

This is used to discover causes of psychological problems (and of course, one does mix the two forms of therapies at times.) Hypno analysis can be summarised briefly as the doctrine of "cause and effect". Every effect (the symptom) must have a cause. Hypno analysis reveals and thus removes the cause, (see section in course on Abreactions), consequently relieves the symptoms.

As mentioned earlier in the course the cause of the problem has been "repressed" with emotion and now from an adult view point the therapy is used to release it with emotion. You see emotional problems respond particularly well to conscious "hypno analysis". The object of analysis is to bring the patient to "a moment of surprising and liberating enlightenment" and one can be fairly confident that a release will be obtained usually within six to twelve sessions of analysis. With these cases we are talking about a complete and lasting release, by finding and removing originating causes, as opposed to mere control of symptoms by suggestions. There is no reason why anyone should put up with something "inside themselves, but outside their control". Providing they are prepared to devote time, money, effort and self discipline to be free of their problem.

The use of conscious hypnosis dramatically speeds up analysis, and similar results can be achieved in a few weeks, which take mainstream psychologists much longer with conventional 100 hour analysis. A question often asked is, can normal people be psychoanalysed? I'd reply, not only can they be, but they should be. For an insight into yourself, it has no equal and as a professional therapist to be, is not only wise to remove any neurosis you yourself may have prior to treating others, but it is also an excellent way to learn the procedures of psycho analysis through the experience of having it done on yourself.

The process used is to get rapport with the client, induce the trance and then deepen the trance. Next it's time for the process of free association, which will be explained more fully in a few moments. The next step is to give the patient some ego strengthening therapy, the major post hypnotic suggestion is then given, that at the next session the patient will instantly and deeply enter trance being able to recall events and memories freely and easily. Lastly, of course, the client is awoken from the trance in the same way as they would be on stage. So, for psycho analysis, the seven step guide to success and release of the patient's problem is:

SEVEN STEPS TO ANALYSIS SUCCESS

Get Rapport
Induce The Trance
Deepen The Trance
Process of Free Association
Ego Strengthening Therapy
Major Post Hypnotic Suggestion
Awaken From The Trance

Whereas in suggestion therapy the seven point guide to success is:

SEVEN STEPS TO SUGGESTION SUCCESS

Get Rapport
Induce The Trance
Deepen The Trance
Ego Strengthening Therapy
Do Necessary Suggestion Therapy
Major Post Hypnotic Suggestion
Awaken Patient from Trance

So basically, for both analysis and suggestion success, all you need to know has been taught earlier on in this course. So I leave it to you to find out from within these pages. Ego Strengthening is quite literally what it says to make the patient feel good and confident about themselves by the use of positive suggestions.

As for the necessary suggestion therapy, I have told you earlier in the course the ways to phrase these.

If a client wants to do something they aren't doing, then suggestions would be given that they can and will achieve or do this. When they are doing something they don't want to, you must give suggestions that they will not and can no longer do that thing in question. Lastly, the last few main things you need to know are with regards to hypno analysis and are the subjects of:

Transference
Counter Transference
Rationalisation
Free Association

I will explain briefly what each of these four things are.

Transference

To cut quite a long story short, this is the phenomenon often experienced by a client in analysis. As they off load memories from the past and numerous emotions surface within them, the patient will often come to regard you as the only person who seems to care about them and this can and often does result in romantic interest from the patient (whether male or female). You as an ethical therapist must not take advantage of this for two reasons.

It would be unethical as emotions are unsettled in the client and this is just a side effect of analysis. If you were to take advantage of the situation to gain sex, which will sometimes be on offer, not only would it be unethical, but as emotions are unsettled in the client, you once having done something, could find yourself being accused of rape by a client whose mind is slightly in a twirl at the time. This has as you'll have seen in the media, occurred to several therapists in the past.

Counter Transference

This is the phenomenon of a therapist starting to feel emotions towards his clients of a sexual or unhealthy for a therapist/client relationship nature. This usually occurs after a client has demonstrated that they are experiencing transference for you the therapist, so be careful you don't fall victim to this, as it can be dangerous for the same reasons as detailed for transference.

Rationalisation

This is, to put it briefly, the process whereby a patient in analysis tries to rationalise with themselves why they are experiencing certain emotions and certain feelings which they at that time, may not want to or may be scared of feeling. It is done out of a fear of finding a solution to the problem as the patient starts to worry that the cause might be something they can't handle. Well, the truth is now from an adult viewpoint, once they come across the memory that triggers off the abreaction and thus the emotional release of the cause to their problem, then not only will the symptoms vanish, but also they, looking at the cause from an older logical adult viewpoint, will see it wasn't their fault and they need not blame themselves for the way they felt at the time.

Free Association

This is the process, whereby once in the hypnotic state, the patient is allowed to freely associate one memory to another in their mind and at the same time tell you what is popping into their minds. Once under hypnosis, you'd tell the patient to just relax and tell you the very first thing that pops into their mind and then to link and connect this to another memory which they must tell you. And so they must go on linking and connecting all memories to other memories which pop into their mind, however unconnected or illogical those memories may seem at the time of recollection to the patient. So the key phrase here is, "link and connect." You, as the therapist take notes of the things said and quite often you'll see a pattern occurring which often indicates to you what the cause of the problem is even before the client has realised and has their moment of enlightening emotional release which ends their problems. It is merely a matter of time before all the memories recalled start to have a lot in common and then soon after an abreaction will occur and the problem will be released with emotion. At this time it is very useful to have a box of tissues handy in your consulting room.

If based on what you have learnt in this course, you feel sooner than spend

£500 on the Neil French course to learn the in depth secrets of analysis, you feel you have enough confidence to start doing analysis now and learn from experience in order to save money. Then I say, although I'd recommend you earn as you learn by doing suggestion therapy first and as you earn study the Neil French Course. I would say if you decide to do this, then an excellent book to buy which will teach you all the rest you need to know about analysis prior to you treating a patient and costs under £10 is the book "A Layman's Guide to Psychiatry and Psycho Analysis," by Doctor Eric Berne. He is also the author of Games People Play and I believe this is published by Penguin and available from the psychology section of your local bookstore.

PART FIFTEEN

THE BIZARRE

A mixture of information introducing you to the subjects of past life regression shows and therapy sessions, U.F.O. and police forensic style investigative hypnosis and ideas for getting rich in the hypnotic industry.

In these next few pages, we shall be exploring a mix of information on several areas of the hypnotic industry which are often never mentioned in training courses such as this. Firstly lets cover the subject of police forensic style hypnosis, which was featured on Paul McKennas Network First documentary during Spring 1995 on ITV. The subject was also covered in The Hypnotists Bible, a book written by my mentor and tutor, Delavar, a respected stage hypnotist and hypnotherapist of over 60 years extensive experience.

Anyway to get down to basics, in the USA, several police forces as were shown on the McKenna show have brought in hypnotherapists in order to uncover the identity of a victims attacker in cases such as rape or assault. The reason that hypnosis can be so useful in circumstances such as these is that being raped or assaulted can be so traumatic to the victim that it becomes too "hot" for the mind to handle. In order to instantly come to terms with things, the memories of the event are repressed into the subconscious mind and as with standard psychotherapy you can make the client relive the event which has been repressed, except this time, as they are under hypnosis they can do it without any emotional or psychological attachment as if they are just watching the event happen as a movie on the TV screen within their minds eye, which of course, is what you instruct them to do.

The only difference between police forensic hypnosis and most psychotherapy is that usually you know there's a problem, but not what it is and as such, it takes several sessions. Whereas with forensic hypnosis you know when the event took place, what happened etc. and where, so you are able to just place the person into a trance and once under hypnosis and having instructed them to experience all they are to remember as just a movie and TV screen in their minds eye, so that they are emotionally unattached from the memory of events. You literally just have to instruct them to go back in their mind, through their memories to the time, place etc. that the event took place and recall everything as a crystal clear technicolour image in their minds eye.

You then just take down the details they give and ask questions to clarify on small points. Remembering of course to always ask open ended questions. As a therapist doing analysis or regression, you must always be careful to ask only open ended questions and never to suggest things that could have happened, either indirectly or directly. For example, if you said, did he put his penis in your mouth? Even if this hadn't taken place, the patient under hypnosis would think that as you had asked the question, it is possible it could have occurred and as such, false memory syndrome could come into play and the patient could recall memories which far from being true, are in fact, the product of direct and/or indirect suggestions made by the therapist. So the rule of thumb in all cases of this nature is the therapist has two ears and one mouth, so should use his ears twice as much to listen. In other words, under analysis you need only say "now link and connect" to the next memory etc. until you become well versed in the subject, be cautious at all times to say anything else to extract information from the hypnotic client. The collected information on the attacker's identity is then used to form a photo fit picture, which can then be used to find the criminal responsible.

Those who have seen the Paul McKenna TV Documentary, will have seen police forensic style hypnosis in action and as such, will know just how successful it is and just how similar the criminals caught who admitted to the offences looked to the pictures compiled from the descriptions given by the victims under hypnosis. So yes, this does work remarkably well.

The last thing I will add here is, that a police artist can be in the room at the same time as was done on the McKenna documentary to compile a sketch drawing of the attacker as the session takes place, the victim is then awoken from trance and when they confirm the picture looks like their attacker, this can be used by the police to find the criminal. Incidentally, I am led to believe, several UK police forces have used this forensic hypnosis method, but as of yet are keeping very quiet about it.

U.F.O. investigative hypnosis is much the same in many ways. Again you must never suggest anything to the client, they must be the ones to offer up information to you and as mostly they will believe they have been abducted by aliens in a U.F.O. you know what event you are regressing them to and as such, you proceed in the same way as getting a victim to recall their attackers identity and let the patient offer up all the information, which of course is recorded by you, so that the client has it to refer to when they are awoken from the trance. There are several U.F.O. societies in the UK and even more in US. Join one of these and you'll meet lots of potential clients for your new services as well as meeting other hypnotists who do U.F.O investigative hypnosis and as such, you can learn tricks of the trade from the horses mouth, so to speak.

The next subject I will discuss is past life regression shows, which were pioneered by a stage hypnotist Mr Julian Caruso of Stoke on Trent. (He can be contacted via Stoke on Trent Yellow Pages.) Should you contact Mr Caruso and discover where his next show is, then you can go and see him in action, which will teach you far more about the format of a past life regression show than anything I could write within these pages. As a past life regression show can be presented quite legitimately for scientific research purposes, no licenses are required and comedy can be injected into the show by you the hypnotist using one liners that relate to the situations the on stage subjects are reliving. These shows are enjoyable, entertaining and educational. As such, they are well attended by the public and can be very lucrative.

The basic course of events is much the same as a normal stage hypnosis show, except that once under, instead of comedy routines you get the on stage subjects to regress to 8 years of age, then to being a baby, then to the birth experience. Next to the womb, then to a past life etc. Each time getting them to relive the memories which they tell you. (Here a microphone is held near to their mouth so audience hear too.) You can then inject comedy lines also to make the evenings events funny and basically that's what the show is made up of. After the show is a great time to get clients for one to one personal past life regression sessions and make even more money out of the shows. So next you need to know how to conduct personal one to one past life regression sessions, which of course, is what I'll be discussing next.

The basics have been covered earlier in the course, basically, you get the client under hypnosis, set the tape recorder running to record any events they recall and then regress them in much the same way as detailed above. Although several patients I have regressed in the past have been featured on TV shows and in magazines, I have very little experience in this area and as such, would advise anyone wishing to conduct regression sessions to go have your own past life regression done by another hypnotist, as you'll learn an awful lot from this. I'd also recommend a book by Mr Richard Webster, entitled "Making Money from Past Life Regression." It's available from Magic Books by Post in Bristol (address earlier in course.) and contains a complete induction script and full instructions on how to conduct a successful past life regression session. For just £30 including postage and packing, this book is a bargain as you'll earn this back many times over in treating clients at around £30 to £45 per one hour session.

As a patient could have had more than one past life, they may wish to explore several of them and so each new client is a potential goldmine in monetary terms. Incidentally, master copies bearing blank spaces for your details are included in the book for publicity materials to promote your new past life regression services. New age shops are ideal places to site your advertising.

To cut a long story short, it is believed that if you have a weak wrist in this life, under regression you might recover memories showing that in a past lifetime you were in a sword fight and your hand was chopped off. When awoken from trance, knowing this information, your injury in this lifetime could disappear and your wrist could be returned to normal strength. The Bridey Murphy case is the most famous case investigated and a book by the same name is available. The leading expert on past life regression is generally regarded to be Miss Ursula Marcum, who has written several excellent books on the subject all of which are available from your local library or bookstore. Anyway, I hope to have given you enough information on the subject so that should you decide regressions are for you then you'll be able to earn as you learn and source all the reference materials you need very quickly.

The next area of the industry I will discuss is the huge income that can be earned from increased sports performance and motivational training. (Both hypnotic and non hypnotic.) With regards to these subjects I say just read Unlimited Power and Awaken the Giant Within, by Anthony Robbins and you will have all the knowledge you need to start offering these services and earning from them. Basically though, under hypnosis, you strengthen their egos, make them feel confident and have them carry out "mental rehearsals" in their mind, in which they see themselves successfully achieving their goals and performing at an increased level. Having done things several times in their minds, the persons subconscious will believe that they have already done this successfully, several times and so will be confident enough to now achieve it in reality.

PART SIXTEEN

COMPLETE MIND THERAPY (CMT)

Well my dear student, our time together is almost at an end, and your initial education in hypnosis is almost complete.

Now the reason I say "initial" education is because you will learn far more from the university of life and through the medium of hands on practical experience than any training course could ever teach you.

That is not to say that your academic study should end. Indeed at the rear of this, the final manual you will find a recommended reading list which you are advised to follow in order to further your studies as you also put the contents of this course to use and therefore start to earn as you learn.

Prior to teaching you the concept and operation of a Complete Mind Therapy session, I would urge you to consider the very true fact that personal hands on training with an experienced expert of their craft is by far the easiest and most effective way of learning a new skill and hypnosis is no exception. Discounted personal one to one training courses with me your head tutor, Jonathan Royle are available in order that you can learn through hands on demonstrations, exercises and experience. Contact www.Magical.co.uk or www.magicalguru.com for more details on this.

Those of you seriously wishing to pursue a career in hypnotherapy are without doubt advised that eight hours in my company (from 10am until 6pm) on the day of your choice would not only be the learning experience of a lifetime but would also be an excellent chance to ask me any questions you may have.

Now without further ado, I shall explain the concept of Complete Mind Therapy. What follows is the structure of a one hour complete mind therapy session, which when followed in this order will produce excellent results at all times.

Use this format for all your one hour long Complete Mind Therapy sessions and due to its unique structure you will be able to treat any and all problems presented to you with just one single one hour session and the audio tape which you give the client on completion of their session.

THE COMPLETE MIND THERAPY SESSION STRUCTURE

Advertise to obtain your clients

Client shows up for session

Get the relevant fee off them now

Obtain rapport over a cup of tea

Obtain total belief and expectancy by your professional office and personal appearance

Ask the client to answer all pre – session questions

Do follow your thumb with your eyes, suggestibility test and anchor the cure to successful completion of this test

Induce trance via physical relaxation method and then counting backwards from 300 method

Deepen trance via staircase of relaxation

Deepen further by image of bed/sleep

Deepen further by dream/blackboard method

Ego strengthening therapy

The Necessary therapy

Anchor good time of life feelings to finger and thumb action

Ruler to 100% confidence

Ruler to 100% willpower

Ruler to 100% self image/esteem

Ruler to 100% relevant to actual problem the client has

T.V set get rid of the past visualisation

Mirror stare to instil new feelings and behaviour as reality

Direct suggestion therapy

Pain and pleasure suggestions

Repeat of direct suggestion therapy

Implant major post hypnotic suggestion

Awaken the client from trance

Give them their tape and any other information

Say goodbye to them and prepare for your next client to arrive

These are the 17 sections which go together to make the whole, which is a Complete Mind Therapy session. The structure is such that we have combined together the most effective elements of counselling skills, psychotherapy, suggestion therapy, aversion therapy, creative visualisation, noesitherapy, sports psychology and in fact all 14 areas which this course teaches are combined with an emphasis on neuro programming or as it is sometimes called neuro associative conditioning (N.A.C.), to give us a one hour long approximately session, which is so effective, that in my personal experience, only one session is necessary to cure the clients problem forever.

If they do need some back up therapy later, they can then of course just listen to the audio tape which you have given them. I shall now explore each of these 17 separate sections which make up the whole and explain how to carry them out for greatest success.

ADVERTISE TO GET CLIENTS

Advertising has been touched on before but here is some further advice. By far the most effective way to obtain clients is by word of mouth advertising, which will be generated for you at no charge by past clients which you have successfully treated, but of course you need some clients first for word of mouth advertising to start happening.

You are advised to obtain a black and white matt finish photograph of yourself, apparently hypnotising someone in the usual clichéd hypnotist manner. This is then sent along with a press release typed in double spaced format on single sided white A4 paper, explaining that after a comprehensive course of study, you are now the ONLY Complete Mind Therapist in your local area able to help people with all their habits, fears, phobias, emotional problems, pain control and other areas. This photograph and press release bearing your contact details are sent to the features editors and news editors of all your local and regional newspapers and magazines, often leading to a large write up promoting your business, which costs you nothing whilst generating lots of clients. This approach can also be used with local and regional radio and TV stations, leading to feature interviews on their news and entertainment shows, which costs you nothing and leads to more clients. Those who are ambitious can do this on a national level with TV radio and press, leading to stardom, appearance fees and more clients for your business. Talk shows such as Kilroy, Trisha, This Morning and many others are always looking for interesting guests and subjects to feature and this may as well be you.

The general rule of thumb is that on a local/regional level you do all TV, radio and media interviews for free. Whilst those on a national level will always involve all your out of pocket and travel expen along with an appearance and/or interview fee being paid to you also.

The next best way to get clients at NO cost is to offer FREE lecture demonstrations of your hypnotic skills to local women's groups, lions clubs, Masonic lodges and other special social clubs of these kinds. Doing these FREE lecture demonstrations costs you nothing and will usually lead to many sales of your audio hypnotherapy tapes on the night and also to bookings for your sessions in person.

Another excellent way to get started at NO cost, is to offer some local venues a FREE stage hypnotism show, which both gives you a chance to rehearse your new stage show and the show itself will lead to paid bookings for other shows, sales of your hypnotherapy tapes on the night and of course, bookings for personal one to one sessions.

Handing your business card to each and every person you meet by way of introduction will rapidly get your name circulated around the community and ultimately lead to many bookings. With business cards available as cheaply as £25 for 1000, from companies advertising in Exchange and Mart, this also is a practically no cost way to get your business kicked off.

Other low cost and effective ways to obtain clients, include having some A5 size leaflets advertising your services printed, then visit all your local libraries and place a folded up leaflet into each and every book on the shelves of the self help, psychology and health sections. People borrowing these kinds of books tend to have problems and/or health complaints they wish to sort out and as such, are red hot leads for you to target, very often leading to bookings.

A classified advert in your local and regional papers, whilst being very cheap to run, can generate 100's of clients, especially if the advert is worded as follows:

FREE HYPNOTHERAPY AND PSYCHOTHERAPY, AVAILABLE FROM ESTABLISHED PROFESSIONAL MIND THERAPIST. FOR FREE SESSION CALL XXXXX XXXXXX. SINCERE HELP FOR ALL PROBLEMS.

This advert of 20 words is placed under the Personal Services section of the classified adverts. As the advert offers the reader a free session, you will get loads of calls and when the potential client calls you explain that most therapists take around three sessions to treat people at an average of £40 per session, which would cost them around £120 at least. However, as a special offer, if they book now, they can have a FREE session of Complete Mind Therapy, which is so powerful and effective that only one session is needed, which immediately saves them around £80 at least. On top of this instant saving, you'll give them the session FREE of charge, just so long as they purchase the back up audio "Hypnotherapy tape" for the special price of just £39.95.

This means you end up getting just 5p less than the normal cost of your sessions anyway and most all callers will book, as they think they are saving lots of money, getting something for FREE and getting a discount on the back up tape. Which means all in all, they feel they are getting a bargain and so book there and then. Believe me, this classified advert offering FREE sessions will generate you your income of a substantial nature on a weekly basis. Each advert placed will pay for itself many times over, so the more local and regional papers you advertise in, the more money you'll make in the shortest space of time possible.

As mentioned before, in the long term, it's worth having a display advert in your local areas Yellow Pages. This display advert, should be as big as those which other therapists are running and there are a few things which will ensure you get all the business. These are, to have a photo of yourself upon the advert as it adds a personal human touch, mention upon the advert your Professional Association memberships, state that you offer FREE Complete Mind Therapy sessions for ALL problems and offer them a FREEPHONE number to call you on. People will always call a freephone number first before paying for a call, especially if it's on the advert offering FREE therapy sessions, which of course, yours will.

The final thing to improve your advert response is to name you business something such as, ABC Hypnotherapy, so that your business appears at the top of the alphabetical list and so is seen first. You are also advised to obtain your FREE lineage entries in both you local Thompson Local Directories, and within the Yellow Pages, as again, this costs nothing for a lineage ad and it does generate some extra enquiries.

It's also worth writing to your regional head office of both B.U.P.A. and your areas N.H.S area healthcare authority, requesting that you are granted a B.U.P.A. and N.H.S. provider number respectively. They will send you all necessary forms and there is no charge to obtain your provider numbers, which once obtained and listed on all promotional materials, helps to attract more clients, as B.U.P.A members will know they can claim on their healthcare insurance to pay for the session. Also doctors will know they can refer people to you on the N.H.S. as you have the N.H.S. provider number. Bearing this in mind, once you have obtained both provider numbers, which costs nothing, it is worthwhile sending a letter of introduction, along with your advertising leaflets, to all the doctors and dentists surgeries in your area, who may then refer clients to you and so increase your business.

A little common sense will reveal numerous other no cost or low cost advertising methods, which do lead to 100's of clients. A last few examples to set you thinking on the right track are as follows:

Place cards on supermarkets "For Sale" boards, using the FREE sessions ploy detailed earlier.

Place cards on newsagents notice boards all over your local area, again using the FREE ploy.

Send leaflets advertising driving test nerves therapy, to all the driving schools and instructors in your area, offering to wholesale them audio hypnotherapy tapes, which they can then sell on at a profit to their clients, thus also helping to increase the level of their pass 1st time success rate, as the students will not be nervous during the test.

Leaflets sent to travel agents, offering cure your fear of flying sessions, with a cover letter pointing out that any clients they obtain for you will cure their fear and so will want to go on a holiday which involves flying, which means the holiday will cost more and so as the travel agent, they will get more commission on the deal which means by being your unpaid salesman they are increasing their own profits.

These are just a few examples of ways to get clients at little or no cost to yourself. But with a little imagination and common sense, 100's of other ways of obtaining clients at little, or no cost to yourself will present themselves to you, if you think along the lines I've already illustrated.

To sum up on advertising, in the rare event of potential clients replying to your adverts and then not booking there and then on the phone, I would suggest you take their name and address and send them your advertising leaflet, by first class post, as quite often, when they receive this, it's enough to spur them into action, so that they do call back and book a session rather than never hearing from them again. One last point is, that by contacting you in the first place, the client has admitted to themselves they have a problem and so are now making a commitment to change things for the better and so they are already 95% of the way to a solution and just need a trigger to success and that is where we therapists come in. We give the client permission to heal them and through the therapy, motivate them to a successful outcome. This combined with the large element of the placebo effect coming into play, as quite simply if they book a session with you, they obviously believe you can help them and expect it to work, or why else would they contact you? Upon taking the booking off the client, take their name, address and telephone number and inform them that if they have to cancel, for any reason, they must give you at least 24 hours notice, or else the full fee will be payable anyway, just like going to the dentist. This stops timewasters and compounds the belief in the clients mind that you're a busy and successful professional. Should they not show up for the session, send them an invoice on a letterhead, headed "Litigation Department", demanding the £39.95 fee and without doubt, you'll get payment by return of post.

CLIENT SHOWS UP FOR SESSION

AND

GET THE RELEVANT FEE OFF THEM

AND

OBTAIN RAPPORT OVER A CUP OF TEA

AND

OBTAIN 100% TOTAL BELIEF/EXPECTANCY

Having booked their session, the client showing up is an important point in their treatment, as they have then made a real commitment to solve their problem. You greet them at your office door and shake them firmly by the hand, whilst looking them directly in the eye, which both gets instant rapport and puts you in control. They see you dressed smartly and professionally which compounds their belief and expectancy levels in your ability to cure them. Having got the client to sit down you say, "Just as when you go to a gypsy, they say cross my palm with silver, well I've got to say cross my palm with £39.95, please, as none of us like talking about money and by getting it all out of the way now, it means we can then concentrate on what's most important today, which is YOU and us solving your problem today."

This both puts them at ease as they perceive your main priority is them and also, it means you've already been paid, which is both a lovely feeling and also a most powerful part of the therapy itself. You see, when the client parts with the money, it's really serious commitment to their own success and concrete's their belief and expectancy levels to a height such that success is 100% guaranteed, as they must believe you can help them and they must expect the treatment to work as why else would they either contact you, book a session, show up and/or pay the fee up front, unless they expect to get the end result of being cured. Bearing this in mind and the power of the placebo effect, combined with the therapeutic power of your caring bedside manner it would almost matter little what treatment you actually gave them now, as the end beneficial result of them being cured would no doubt be the same anyway, however, the CMT session, which they receive, is so powerful and effective in its therapeutic content, that success is 100% guaranteed, if the clients belief and expectancy levels are total.

The diplomas they see hanging on your office wall, together with the book shelf of impressive looking psychology books, all compound the belief and expectancy thing even further. Your office should contain a black leather reclining chair for the client to lie in, a black directors chair for you to sit in at your desk, upon which should be a desk lamp. Your diplomas are displayed, framed upon the wall and you have 2 tape recorders, one of which is positioned behind the clients chair will play the relaxation music for the session later, whilst at the same time, the one upon your desk, to which is connected a microphone, records the entire session from the point of asking the client to close their eyes and starting the induction, until having awoken the client, which should be 45 minutes maximum, so one side of a 90 minute tape will be sufficient and as your voice and background music are picked up by the microphone the end result is a tape which bears your voice over the top of the relaxation music which will be highly effective when listened to. Giving the client a cup of tea instantly puts them at ease and helps relax them and then you can answer their general questions prior to moving onto asking them the pre-session questionnaire, which follows:

ASK CLIENT LIST OF 16 PRE-SESSION QUESTIONS

What follows are the 16 questions which you ask the client to answer, honestly, directly and in detail, before you start the actual hypnotic induction process. The answers given will help you carry out the session with the greatest of success for the reasons detailed after each listed question that follows. The fact you use their answers, which are personal to them, as part of the therapy makes the session seem far more personal to them, especially as you try to use their name a lot, as a persons name is, to them, the sweetest thing in the entire English language. It also means that as you feed the personal information they have given to us by the questions asked back to them as part of the therapy as it is personal to them and they can relate to it so well this explains why the concept of Complete Mind Therapy is so successful. The 16 questions to ask are as follows:

What is your name?

This is so we can call them by their first name throughout the session

Your address please?

This is just for future reference, as in future you may wish to contact clients to see if they will participate in TV and/or radio show broadcasts.

You telephone number?

Again just for reference as in question 2

Your date of birth?

By knowing this, we can work out the clients age. (Never ask their age outright).

What's their problem?

Obviously asked so we know what we're treating

How long have you had this problem?

Using this piece of information and the clients D.O.B. we can work out what age the client was when the problem started

How do you feel this problem started?

Whilst the way they feel the problem started may not exactly be correct, just so long as it's what they at this time consciously believe to be correct, then we can use this information to erase connections with the past during therapy.

What do you feel I need to do for you today to permanently cure this problem?

Again the answer they give, however daft, will when acted upon, provide the ideal way to cure the patient. This is because, if they feel doing XYZ would cure them, then they believe that if you did XYZ they would be cured. So by doing XYZ they will be cured, as this is what they have convinced themselves needs to be done for a cure to be achieved.

What is the final outcome you wish to achieve from today?

Whilst you may think, for example, that a smoker would say to stop smoking in reply to this question, this is not always the case. They could just as easily say that by stopping smoking today they wish to become healthier and be able to go swimming again like they used to. In other words, the answer to this question very often reveals something we can feed back to them later as an incentive to achieve their goals.

What was the best experience of you entire life, a time you felt confident, proud, loved and on top of the world?

Their answer is later used for the finger and thumb good times feeling connection technique.

What was the worst and most emotionally painful experience of your entire life?

This answer can be used later in the pain/pleasure section of therapy by having them imagine how they felt then etc. and linking it to the thought that any continuance of past actions will make them feel just as bad as they did then whereas avoidance of past actions makes them feel as good as, if not better as their reply to question 10

Who's the one person you love most in the entire world?

By getting the persons name, you can refer to them directly during the pain/pleasure section of the therapy by way of having the client imagine how upsetting it would be to this named person they love so much if they were to have continued smoking and killing themselves. Until they saw each other no more or indeed if the habit/problem had continued making them so stressed and anxious that the person they loved so much feels driven away from them and grows to hate them. As the client loves this person so much there will be strong emotional connection with any thoughts about this person and needless to say the client will wish to avoid upsetting them at all costs and because of the scenario just given to them, the only way to avoid upsetting them as far as their subconscious mind is concerned is by ending their habit/problem etc. once and for all.

Are you on any medication for this problem?

Here, a copy of the medical reference book PIMMS is useful, as you can look up the drugs name, revealing exactly what the drug is prescribed for, what its side effects are and indeed, by having prescribed it, what the clients medical GP seems to think the real problem is, which may not always be the same as that being presented to us by the client and so we can ensure our therapy targets the correct problem as well as the clients perceived problem if necessary.

Is there a history of this problem within your direct family?

This really just gives us more of an idea why this client has got this particular problem in the first place
Have you tried any other alternative therapies to cure this problem before?

If they answer yes, ask which and then make it clear to the client that the treatment you will give them is the most powerful and effective of its kind. Hence it's called Complete Mind Therapy. This is done to remove any doubts they may have instilled in them due to past failures and helps to concrete their belief and expectancy levels in the treatment working 100%

Have you got any questions for me before we begin?

Should the client have any questions, it's just a matter of using your common sense to answer in a manner which puts their mind at ease and ensures they totally believe this treatment will change their life.

Then you get the client to sign and date the bottom of the questionnaire below a printed statement, which says:

I (THEIR NAME HERE) OF (THEIR ADDRESS) DO HEREBY DECLARE I AM OVER 18 YEARS OF AGE AND CONSENT TO (YOUR NAME) TREATING ME WITH HYPNOSIS AND COMPLETE MIND THERAPY.

Once the client has signed such a statement it will be far harder for any legal claims to be made against you for malpractice. Where wishing to treat children and/or those under the age of 18 you must have their parent sign a statement saying:

I (THEIR NAME) OF (THEIR ADDRESS) DO HEREBY DECLARE I AM THE LEGAL PARENT/GARDIAN OF (CLIENTS NAME) AND DO HEREBY GIVE MY CONSENT FOR (YOUR NAME) TO TREAT

THEM WITH HYPNOSIS AND COMPLETE MIND THERAPY.

Again this is done to cover you 100% legally, as without proof of parent or guardians consent it is illegal to hypnotise these people under 18 years.

DO FOLLOW YOUR THUMB WITH EYES TEST AND ANCHOR THE CURE TO SUCCESSFUL COMPLETION

Here, you get the client to stand upright, feet together, left arm down by their side, right arm stretched out in front of them and right hand clenched into a fist, with their right thumb stuck up directly into the air. You tell the client that on the count of 3 you want them to move their right arm around in a clockwise direction as far as they comfortably can, without moving their feet from the position they are currently in. They are told to stare at their thumb at all times, whilst doing this and indeed should tell you when they have reached the point where it becomes uncomfortable to move any further. You then count to 3 and the client does as they've been told and when they reach the point where they can move no further, you ask them to stare past their thumb and tell you what they can see in the background in line with their thumb, which can act as a marker to how far they got this first time. The client is then told to resume their original position and then told to close their eyes and keep their arm exactly where it is until you say otherwise. You ask the clients to imagine in their minds eye as 100% total reality, that they are once again rotating their body from the hips in a clockwise direction whilst staring at their thumb just like before. However, as anything is possible in their imagination, you want them to imagine being able to move considerably further than before, both without discomfort and with the greatest of ease and they are told to tell you when they have gone further in their minds eye than they previously did in reality. The client is then told something such as:

"Well (their name) that's excellent, you have just achieved something which was once so difficult in a way which has proved so ridiculously easy, thanks to the power of your mind. Now, (their name), believe it or not, if you've used your powers of intelligence, imagination and concentration effectively, then for you this will have become 100% total reality. So on the count of 3 I'd like you to re-open your eyes and repeat the test by rotating your body as far as you comfortably can in a clockwise manner and as you do so, on the count of 3, notice how as those imagined thoughts of but a few seconds ago become a reality for you, how your goal of solving (their problem) which you once thought would be difficult to achieve will also prove to be so ridiculously easy."

You then count to 3, they repeat it again for real and I guarantee you that without fail, the client will be able to move considerably further this time than they did the first time around and as they see with their own eyes, their thoughts of but a few seconds ago become a physical reality, so they come to believe as 100% total reality that the treatment you are about to give them will work and so they are now 99% of the way to solving their problem.

INDUCE TRANCE VIA PHYSICAL RELAXATION AND COUNTING BACKWORDS FROM 300 METHOD

It's now time to get the client to sit down, to close their eyes and to begin breathing deeply and regularly in through their nose and then out through their mouth, as they continue to relax etc., etc. At this point the relaxation music is turned on and you start to record the session, thus making their "back-up" therapy tape as the session continues. You explain to the client that you will mention areas of their body and that upon doing so, you want them to physically tense up all the muscle groups in that body area, whilst at the same time in their minds eye, imagining 2 pieces of rope tied together in knots and that these knots represent the stresses, tensions, fears, and upsets of days and weeks gone by, which are stored in the muscle groups they are physically tensing. Then the client is told you will count from 3 to 1 and that on 1 when you snap your fingers like this (do it as example) they are to instantly relax the muscle groups they were tensing, whilst at the same time imagining as 100% total reality, in their minds eye, that with your click of the fingers the 2 ropes in their minds eye instantly separate. As they instantly untie, so as they become separate pieces of rope, so in reality all muscles in their body becoming so limp, so loose, so relaxed, so heavy and so tired. They are then asked to nod their head if they understand. Then you proceed to do as just stated for the following muscle groups in this order:

A   The feet and ankles
B   Lower leg area and knees
C   Upper leg area and hips

D   Stomach and abdomen
E   Chest area
F   The back and spine
G   Finger tips to wrists
H   Every muscle from wrist to elbows to shoulders
I   The shoulders and shoulder blades
J   The neck area
K   The jaw and cheek muscles
L   The eyelids and forehead

When you've gone through this list and the client, who is listening both to your voice and the background music, has physically tensed up and then physically relaxed all these muscle groups from head to toe, they will, I assure you, feel genuinely relaxed in a physical way, especially as your office will be nice and warm and the room will be dimly lit by only your desk lamp at this point. On top of this the visual imagery of the knots untying helps them to achieve psychological relaxation also, and with both a relaxed mind and body, they are in an ideal state for the therapy to be 100% successful. As you go through the 12 point list of muscle groups, you can link from one group to the next with a phrase such as, "with every breath you take, every noise you hear and every word I say, you relax even more. With each second that passes by." This, along with the "standard phrases" as detailed earlier in this course, both help to link nicely from one muscle group to the next and also help to deepen both the physical and psychological levels of the clients relaxation. It can also be good to suggest to them that as each muscle group relaxes, so a feeling of warmth and total relaxation floods their entire body. Having gone through their entire body's muscle groups, you then immediately ask them to start counting backwards from 300 in their minds eye, as you continue to suggest things to them and then link into the induction method as explained in the verbal psychology section, being that of a "subliminal" nature.

DEEPEN VIA STAIRCASE

After continuing with the "subliminal" induction, it's time to deepen the level of trance, here we use the staircase of relaxation as detailed earlier in the course. The client being told that as you count backwards from 10 down to 1, so in their minds eye they will take another step down the staircase they can now see and as this is a staircase of relaxation, they will sink 100 times deeper with each step down they take. Then using the "standard phrases" whilst counting backwards from 10 down to 1 the trance is deepened.

DEEPEN FURTHER BY IMAGE OF BED

Upon reaching the count of 1 with the staircase deepening, it is suggested to the client that at the bottom of the staircase is a beautifully relaxing and comfortable bed into which they are to climb, snuggle up and go fast to sleep, allowing their mind to wander free, allowing your voice to become but a distant sound as they go deeper and deeper to sleep.

DEEPEN FURTHER BY BLACKBOARD

Now tell the client:

"Your now so deeply relaxed and so deeply asleep, that whatever I tell you to do, you would do for your own good and whatever I tell you will happen, will happen again for your own good. However, in order that the work we do together today will be 100% successful in every way, we need your subconscious mind to take you to a level of deep satisfying relaxation, of both mind and body, which will be right for you. Just as your subconscious can be trusted to circulate the blood around your body 24 hours a day, so it can be trusted to take you to a level of relaxation which is going to be for you 100% successful in every way. So I'd like you to…."

You then get the client to imagine that as they've gone to sleep in the bed, they will start dreaming and as they do, they are to dream they are in a classroom, in which is a large blackboard, upon which their name is written in chalk. They are told that in dreamland, when the blackboard is blank they are instantly taken to a depth of relaxation where they can achieve anything and then they are told to imagine rubbing their name out from the blackboard, so that each chalk letter, one by one, is rubbed out and as each letter disappears, so their level of relaxation doubles in every way, until they rub out the last letter. When they relax so completely that your work together today will prove 100% successful as an automatic reflex action.

EGO STRENGTHENING THERAPY

This is where, as detailed in an earlier section of the course, we praise the clients ego, make them feel good about the work you are about to do together and make them believe they are such a wonderful client, with such good powers of intelligence, imagination and concentration, that their success in achieving their goals and aims is 100% assured.

THE NECESSARY THERAPY

A   GOOD FEELINGS FINGER AND THUMB ANCHOR

This technique is to remind the client of the most special and pleasurable time of their life. (See answers to 16 pre-session questions). Tell them then to push the tip of their right forefinger against the tip of their right thumb, thus making a ring, a ring of confidence. As they continue to push their finger and thumb firmly together, they are to notice how confident they feel at that past time, they are to notice how calm and relaxed they feel, how full of will power and ability to achieve anything they are and how, in fact, life seemed so wonderful at the time. They are then told to let go of the image as they separate their finger and thumb. You then tell them that any time from this moment forward, when they feel a little unsure about continuing in their new life as (opposite of what their problem was) they just need to press their finger and thumb together to make the ring of confidence. This will immediately flood their mind and body with all those positive, pleasurable feelings of the past that continuing with their goal will become so ridiculously easy.   This incidentally, is called anchoring, as we have "anchored" a thought to a physical action

B   RULER TO 100% CONFIDENCE
C   RULER TO 100% WILLPOWER
D   RULER TO 100% SELF IMAGE/ESTEEM
E   RULER TO 100% RELEVANT TO PROBLEM

The ruler technique is to have the client imagine a ruler in their minds eye and that upon this are the numbers from 1 to 100%. With 100% being the most desirable level to be at in order to achieve everything and anything.

It is if you like a measuring stick of confidence or of willpower or of self esteem, or whichever is relevant at the time. But for this example we'll use confidence, you tell them it's a measuring stick of confidence and that it's filled with liquid mercury, just like a thermometer is and that if they take a closer look, they can see then tell us at what level from between 1 to 100% their confidence levels are now at, as this is where the mercury level will be. When they have answered with a percentage, we tell them that they need to be at 100% to achieve their aim with 100% success. So they are to imagine heating up the mercury with a very hot lighter flame, until it's become so hot that it has rapidly risen to 100%, at which point they should indicate by saying yes. You then have them imagine taking a hammer and a nail and hammering the nail through the mercury mark at 100% and through the measuring stick, so that their confidence levels are now permanently locked in place at 100% and can never again fall below this level. Once they've done this you tell them to think of the next ruler, which represents their levels of willpower, then the next ruler, which represents their self-image/esteem and how they feel about themselves. Finally the ruler which, using your common sense, you make 100% relevant to each client's particular problem. In all 4 cases, however, the bizarre mental images are used to get the levels to 100% so that 100% success can be achieved. Don't forget that the more bizarre a mental image is, the more effectively it will be acted upon. Lastly, with reference to the ruler relevant to each client's personal problem, use your common sense, but for example, people wishing to pass their driving test, could have a ruler of nerves control, which means that when it's at 100% they are 100% in control of their nerves and so can pass the test.

F   TV SET GET RID OF PAST VISUALISATION

Here, we get the client to imagine watching a TV set in their minds eye, upon which they are watching themselves as they once were. The volume is still very loud, the colour is very bright and all in all, it's very much a reminder of how they once were, which they no longer need. So first, they are to imagine turning the colour down so low that they can no longer see the picture of themselves as they once were. Then they are to turn the volume down, so much that they can no longer hear how they once were. Now that they can neither see nor hear how they once were, they are to turn the TV set off and once switched off, they are to unplug it from the wall, so it can no longer be fed any power to survive as it once was and lastly as they can no longer see, hear or be as they once were, they are to destroy the TV set in their minds eye, by blowing it up with a huge bomb. As they imagine the TV set blowing up, they are to wave goodbye to how they once felt, how they once acted and what they once did, which is no longer part of their everyday reality.

G   MIRROR STARE TO INSTILL NEW FEELINGS/FUTURE AS REALITY

Having got rid of the past, we now need to instill the future and the client's new reality. They are to imagine staring into a full length mirror, in which they can see themselves as they now are, as a (here insert what they wished to achieve). They are to notice how good they feel within themselves, they are to notice how proud they are feeling as they have now achieved their goal and ambition. They are to notice how much better they look, how much better they feel now they are a confident, happy, healthy, calm and relaxed person with bags of willpower, who has now become a (here what it was they wish to achieve). They are then to imagine turning a key in the frame of the mirror, which freezes the reflection in place forever and just so long as this image remains frozen in place so they will continue to be a (here what the aim is).

H   DIRECT SUGGESTION THERAPY

Here common sense is used; the direct suggestions must suggest clearly that the client has achieved their aim. Examples of direct suggestions are contained within the script outlines given within the advanced hypnotherapy chapter. But in short, clients who want to stop doing something they do now, must be told that they have stopped doing it. Whereas clients who wish to do something they don't currently do, must be told they have started to do it, with the greatest of ease.

I   PAIN AND PLEASURE SUGGESTIONS

Here the principle is to reverse the pain and pleasure connectors in the clients mind. So that by so doing, their behaviour is reversed to that they desire and because the cause of the problem which is the pain and pleasure circuit in their mind relevant to their problem has been reversed. The cause of the problem has effectively been removed and so a cure achieved without the need for long sessions of psychotherapy treatment. Thus getting the same end results within one 1 hour session. Also, as the cause has indirectly been dealt with and removed, there is no chance of symptom substitution, so the client you've stopped smoking has no debris left in his/her mind, which could for example, then cause them to start biting their nails instead.

The 3 steps of pain/pleasure therapy are:

Get the client to imagine how they were when they had the problem and in their mind connect this to the most awful experience of their life, in order that it becomes painful for the client to think about or continue being as they once were, because it now has painful associations with this awful real life event of the past. (See their answers to questions.)

Get the client to imagine how they are now, without the problems of the past and in their mind get them to connect this with the most pleasurable experience of their entire life, so it becomes pleasurable to continue with their new behaviour pattern. Because as they continue with the new behaviour pattern, they are always reminded of this very pleasurable past event and feel just as they did then.

Have them think of the person they said they loved most and use the example I gave earlier, of how if they had continued with their problem, they would have ended up dead and/or pushing this loved one away. Either way, the idea is to make it so upsetting to continue with past behaviour, as by doing so, it would remind them that it would upset the one they love so dearly in a way they wish to avoid and so a strong emotional motivating link is made here.

J   REPEAT DIRECT SUGGESTIONS

Prior to implanting post hypnotic suggestion the direct suggestions are repeated to the client once more.

MAJOR POST HYPNOTIC

Here it is suggested to the client, that everything you have said to them, will remain with them for the rest of their lives and will grow stronger with each second that passes by, from this moment forward. Also they will find that each and every time they listen to the audio tape you will give them, it will be just as, if not more effective, than if you were with them in the room in person at the time of listening to it.

AWAKEN CLIENT FROM TRANCE

Here counting up from 1 to 10, you awaken the client, an ideal therapy awakening is:

On 1 – everything I've suggested to you, growing stronger with each second of each minute of each day of each week of each month and of each year for the rest of your life.

On 2 – from this moment forward you will continue with you new desirable lifestyle as an automatic reflex action as 100% total reality.

As on 3 – from this day forward, you will awaken with an inner warm glow of confidence, a renewed optimism to life and by far a more positive attitude to get things done, whilst also continuing in your new lifestyle, as a confident, happy, healthy, calm and relaxed (their aim here)

As on 4 – finding that each day you have a huge inner reservoir of willpower which can be drawn upon when ever needed and which in fact, you will draw upon as an automatic reflex action whenever that little extra help is needed.

As on 5 – every day in every way, things are getting better and better.

As on 6 – something you once thought would be so difficult to achieve has turned out to be so ridiculously easy.

As on 7 – almost as though each and every muscle group in your body is being filled with energy, vitality, confidence and optimism.

As on 8 – almost as though your whole body is being washed in cool refreshing spring water.

As on 9 – lighter and brighter, coming on up out of it.

And on 10 – wakey, wakey rise and shine.

GIVE THEM TAPE ETC.

They are now awake and so you give them the audio tape of the session, along with an instruction sheet, clearly stating that to ensure 100% guaranteed success, they must listen, (but not whilst driving) to the tape every other day, for the next 28 days. In other words, the day after the session they don't, the next day they do and then it's do a day and miss a day for the next 28 days, as it takes 28 days for new habits to be formed and concreted into the human mind. This also puts the onus on them to commit time to their own success and seems to attach so much importance to the tape that A. they will listen to it as instructed and B. the tape will prove to be just as effective as if you were there with them in person.

SAY GOODBYE TO THEM

It's then time to say goodbye to them and await arrival of next client.

This format is followed 100% to the letter for all problems presented to you, with the only minor changes being as follows.

FOR;

***Habits, emotional problems, general nervous complaints etc.**

These kinds of problems are such that the CMT session is conducted 100% to the letter as per example given.

***Fears and Phobias**

Here, instead of using direct suggestions twice, the first time you get the client to imagine what they used to be scared of and then you have them make it an object of ridicule. So that the thought of what once scared them now makes them think humorous thoughts making them laugh and as laughter leads to relaxation, they will then feel relaxed when presented with what once scared them. The more ridiculous and bizarre the mental image is that you get them to imagine in order to make the original fear trigger an object of ridicule, by far the more powerful it will be. For example, a person once scared of spiders is told to dress them in wellies, put a silly party hat on it, a big clowns red nose, a bright silly coat and so on, until the image which was once the trigger to their fear becomes so ridiculous, that all that image can now trigger is laughter and/or relaxation. The rest of the session remains the same.

*Sports psychology/peak performance

Where the first set of direct suggestions normally go, we instead have the client run through a successful mental rehearsal of the increased success they wish to achieve in their sport and/or work. For example, mentally we would take a football player through the full match in a matter of a few minutes and as we did, we would have him imagine as reality scoring more goals than ever before. We would have him feel how it feels to be an achiever and we would make him believe in his mind that he had already successfully achieved his aim and so to do it again would be easy. This works and to illustrate, think of Roger Bannister, who first ran the four minute mile, until then no one had got close, but Roger believed he could do it and so he made it his reality and guess what? Once other athletes had seen Roger achieve something they once believed to be impossible, they knew it could be done and within days of Roger having done it athletes the world over found themselves able to run the four minute mile. Such is the power of belief and mental rehearsals.

*Pain control

Again the only change is that instead of direct suggestion, you instead run through instilling the saliva leads to no pain trigger as detailed in the Noesitherapy chapter. With it here being done whilst the client is in trance and then at the end of the session, the client is reminded to get saliva on their tongue and make the affirmations whenever they need instant pain control in the future.

*Illness and disease

Instead of direct suggestion number one, the client is told to visualise a rabbit in their minds eye in a field filled with 1000's of carrots. These carrots are cancer carrots, AIDS carrots or whatever their illness is carrots.

They are to imagine the rabbit is so hungry and never loses his appetite and he is rapidly eating up all the carrots, one by one and with each carrot the rabbit eats, so in turn as 100% total reality, the cancer, AIDS virus or whatever, is growing weaker and so in turn they are becoming healthier and healthier.

***Stress Management**

Instead of direct suggestions twice, the first time the client is told to visualise the burning fire within them that has got too hot to handle. Then they must imagine connecting a hose to a tap and aiming it at the fire so to keep it cool. Although it continues to burn it will be at a level where the client will be able to deal with challenges which may arise. Or you can the Noesitherapy fight/flight saliva method. Not for pain control, but rather for stress control and instant relaxation.

***Allergies**

Instead of direct suggestion on two occasions, the first time get your client to visualise a Perspex screen across the room and see a clone of themselves becoming "one".

A SUMMARY OF THE KEY POINTS

The more bizarre the images, the more effective they will be.

The subconscious is abstract and is best reprogrammed through images and not just words.

Phrasing suggestions to the subject (are they a visual, auditory, sensual person) helps.

Using their name helps a lot.

Pain/Pleasure and Fight/Flight is the secret.

The CMT session combines all the major areas of hypno/psycho related subjects.

Give them a tape at the end of the session.

NON SPECIFIC TREATMENT SCRIPT
© *2002 JONATHAN ROYLE*

PROCEED AS FOLLOWS:

1) Use the Progressive Relaxation Induction (PRI) as detailed in CMT course and mentioned again in chapter 21 of CMT course!

2) Towards the end of this Induction say the "Post Hypnotic" of **"AND JUST SLEEP NOW!"**

3) Deepen the trance via the staircase visualization method as detailed in chapter 21 of CMT.

4) Deepen further using get into bed and go to sleep visualization, again detailed in chapter 21.

5) Further deepen using having a dream and wiping your name off the blackboard method as per chapter 21.

6) Say the "Post Hypnotic" again of **"AND JUST SLEEP NOW"**

Then its time for step 07 – Ego strengthening Therapy:

As you relax more completely with every breath that you take, every noise that you hear, every word that I say and every second that passes by, You are now so deeply relaxed, so deeply asleep, that whatever I tell you to do, you WILL do for your own good. And whatever I tell you WILL happen, WILL happen for your own good.   Because from this moment forward I am talking directly to your subconscious mind and as you relax more deeply with each word I say and every thought that you think, so in turn every suggestion that I give you, WILL for your own good become 100% Total Reality. You have made a promise to yourself and as you relax more deeply with each second that passes by, so you realize that whilst on the odd occasion it may be OK to break a promise to a friend, that in reality you can NEVER break a promise to yourself. In fact your subconscious mind WILL NOT allow you to break a promise to yourself, you can have 100% faith that your subconscious mind will enable you to achieve everything that I am suggesting to you with the greatest of ease. And as you go deeper and deeper, you notice that the deeper you go, the better you feel and the better you feel, the deeper you will go as you realize now that you can trust your subconscious mind, for just as it makes you breath automatically without any conscious effort, and just as it pumps the blood around your body and keeps you alive, so you can be certain that from this very moment forward your subconscious mind will ensure that every single thing I suggest to you, WILL become your new reality as an automatic reflex action, with the greatest of ease. In fact you will find that something you once thought may be so difficult to achieve will now become so ridiculously easy, as you realize that from this moment forward, you can equal the greatest achievements of life's greatest achievers and that for you, your innermost dreams can and have now become your 100% total reality. Noticing now that with every breath that you take, every noise that you hear and every word that I say, that all the stresses, tensions, worries, fears and apprehensions of days and weeks gone by are leaving your mind and leaving your body NOW!

7)   <u>– NOW TIME FOR THERAPY SPECIFIC TO PROBLEM</u>

Realizing now that from this moment forward, each morning you will awaken with an inner warm glow of confidence, a renewed optimism to life, a more positive attitude to get things done. You will notice that every day in every way you find it so much easier to deal with events and situations, which once would have bothered you greatly. Realizing now that from this moment forward within you is a large inner reservoir of willpower, self-confidence and self-esteem, which you may draw upon as an automatic reflex action whenever you need to, enabling you to deal with everything and anything there and then, the very moment it happens, you no longer need, want, crave or desire for stressful situations and as such from this moment forward with every breath that you take, you will be able to handle everything and anything that life presents to you with the greatest of ease. Nothing bothers you as it once did and in fact you now realize that just as all of the stresses, tensions, Worries, fears and apprehensions of days, weeks, months and years gone by are leaving your body and leaving your mind NOW! So you realize also that every day in every way your life is getting better and better, your approach and attitude to life is getting more relaxed, more positive and more constructive and in turn your approach, attitude and response to other people, especially those you care for, those you respect and those close to you, WILL BECOME far more positive, far more relaxed and far more friendly and appreciative in every way, shape and form. You realize now as 100% Total Reality that your life is now like a mirror, and whatever you give out to others in life is now reflected back towards you tenfold. So from this moment forward as an automatic reflex action you will find that you will send out positive, peaceful, constructive and loving thoughts, actions and words to all those around you and in turn these things will positively and beneficially be reflected back to you tenfold with each second that passes by. Notice how good it feels to realize that these improvements in your daily life have now taken place and will continue to grow stronger and more positive each and every day. Realizing now that just as you can and WILL now equal the greatest achievements of life's greatest achievers, so in turn you now realize that no one person ever did it all alone and so from this moment forward you will eagerly, happily and positively encourage those around you to help in your aims, actions & desires. You no longer resent or feel shy or in any way negative about accepting help, advice and assistance from others, in fact it makes you happy and proud to know that you can enabling you to achieve whatever you wish to achieve with the greatest of ease. Just as you yourself are a wonderful, valuable and worthy person so you now WILL realize from this moment forward, that the opinions of others, especially those of people you respect, people you love and those close to you are worth listening and responding to in a positive manner, just as your opinions and thoughts WILL NOW BECOME and will remain equally Honest, positive, constructive and worthwhile as all the stresses, tensions, worries, fears and apprehensions of every day situations which once would have bothered you have now become and will continue to be but distant memories and things of the past, as from this moment forward you will awaken each morning with an inner warm glow of confidence, a renewed optimism to life, a more positive attitude to get things done and every day in every way you will now realize that you have within you a large inner reservoir of willpower, self-confidence, self-esteem and patience which you can and you will draw upon as a 100% Total Reality automatic reflex action whenever you find yourself in a situation which once would have bothered you. Realizing now that you reap what you sow in life and as such from this moment forward all the stresses, tensions, worries, fears, apprehensions and obsessions which once may have bothered you are now but distant memories and things of the past as you now continue your life as the Confident, Happy, Healthy, Relaxed Stress free positive minded, Loving, caring, considerate individual that you have now become and will continue to be for the rest of your life, with each and every suggestion growing stronger each second of each minute of each hour of each day from this moment forward, you now realize how short life is and how valuable every second of it has now become to you. You no longer need, want, crave or desire to waste a single moment of your now positively Happy, Healthy, Calm and relaxed lifestyle, instead you now wish to and as a result WILL savor every moment, you now notice more closely how enjoyable it is to be in the company of friends, those you respect, Loved ones and others close to you. Their company, their opinions, their honesty, their help, assistance, advice, love and encouragement are all invaluable to you and as a result you WILL RESPOND to them with the same Honesty, Openness, Positiveness, Warmth, Encouragement and Love in all that you do and at all times you spend together. Your greatest achievement in life now being that you have now become one of those rare few, but very talented and perceptive people who is able to admit their own faults and by so doing grow stronger and happier as an individual and as part of a Loving partnership, in short from this moment forward to you the Past is the Past and what you now find is most important to you is The Future, your positive, happy, healthy, confident, relaxed Future made even more enjoyable, positive and beneficial by those around you who are friends, those who Love you, those who respect you and those who care about you which in turn you will reflect back to them as you continue now to live your life like a mirror and reflect to others the way you wish to be Loved for, Cared for, Respected and assisted in your every day life, which from this moment forward is that of a confident, peaceful, happy, healthy, relaxed, stress free, positive thinking, Loving, caring and considerate worthwhile individual.

<u>08)- FINGER & THUMB RING OF CONFIDENCE.</u>

Noticing now that the deeper you go, the better you feel and the better you feel the deeper you will go with every breath that you take, every noise that you hear and every word that I say, as you now allow your mind to wander free as you continue to go deeper down into the world of your dreams and the world of your imagination I want you to imagine and remember that one time in your life when you felt more Happy, more confident, more proud and on top of the world than you have ever done before. It could have been a time when you won an award or just a time on Holiday when you felt you could achieve anything, it matters not just so long as YOU NOW FEEL Happy, Healthy, Relaxed, Calm, Confident & Loving to yourself and to others in everyday life enabling you to live a 100% fulfilling and stress free lifestyle. Now I just want to notice how good it feels to experience these positive and beneficial states of mind and body and as you do realize now that whenever you need to renter this special place in your every day life, whenever you are confronted with the unexpected or those things which once would have bothered or concerned you then now as an automatic reflex action all you need do is push together the tip of your forefinger of the right hand together with the tip of your thumb and instantly this will make your ring of confidence, your ring of willpower, your ring of self-esteem and your ring of patience that will instantly enable you to remain as the Calm, Confident, Happy, Healthy, Relaxed and Loving individual that you have now become and will continue to be from this moment forward. Remembering that your subconscious will remind you as an automatic reflex action to make this ring of confidence with your finger and thumb as and when you need that little extra help in every day life. As you relax deeper and deeper with each second that passes by and every word that I say.

<u>09- RULERS OF CONFIDENCE, WILLPOWER, SELF-IMAGE/ESTEEM, PATIENCE & TRUST.</u>

Realizing now that the personal attributes of self-confidence, Willpower, Positive Self-esteem, Patience and Trust are the only attributes that any individual needs in every day life to remain as a Confident, Happy, Healthy, Relaxed and Loving person, Just as you have now become and continue to be as you live your stress free lifestyle every day in every way getting better and better. So I'd Like you to imagine a thermometer in your minds eye with the numbers from 0 to 100% on it and within this thermometer the level at which the mercury is indicates the level at which your personal levels of self-confidence, Will Power, self-esteem, Patience and Trust are currently at. As you relax more completely with each second that passes by I want you to notice the level that the mercury is currently at and then realize that if we raise the level to 100% then any and all problems you may once have had in your life will no longer ever be able to bother you or effect you and as you realize this as 100% Total Reality I'd like you to imagine heating up the mercury in the thermometer with a lighter or a hot flaming candle so that the mercury gets hotter and hotter, so hot in fact that it starts to rise up inside the thermometer. Up past 30%, up past 40 & 50%, all the way up and past 80% and then notice and just realize in your minds eye that the mercury has now reached 100% and as you notice this realize how much more confident you feel, how you realize now your Willpower is also at a 100%, your self-esteem is higher than it ever has been at 100% and your Patience and trust both of yourself and others is now also at 100% making you a much happier, healthier, relaxed, calm and loving person in every way as you continue to live a stressfree lifestyle. Realizing now that in order to feel this confident forever we need to fix the mercury in place at 100% so imagine now in your minds eye that you have a hammer and a nail and that you are now hammering the nail through the thermometer and through the mercury at the 100% level and rather than leaking out the mercury is now being fixed, solidly, permanently in place so that from this moment forward your levels of self-confidence, Will Power, self-esteem, Patience and Trust are now fixed at 100% enabling you to live your life as the Happy, healthy, Confident, Relaxed, Calm, Loving & trusting individual that you have become and now continue to be as all areas of your life benefit immensely from these improvements every day in every way.

10- TV SET GET RID OF PAST

As you relax and go deeper, so the deeper you go the better you will feel and the better you feel the deeper you will go as you now imagine in your minds eye a TV set upon which you can see an image of how you once were, just see it clearly on the TV screen the person you once were, notice all those things about yourself that both you and others disliked which are no longer part of you and realize now these things have become and must now remain part of the past. And as you realize this its time to turn down the volume on the TV so imagine doing this now, then just imagine turning down the Colour and contrast so that the image of how you once were disappears completely and now as we realize that image has gone forever, we no longer need the TV set switched on so imagine turning it off, yes that's perfect and now as you relax more just imagine unplugging the TV set from the wall and as you do realizing that you yourself have now said goodbye completely to the past and how you once were as finally just imagine blowing up the TV set with a large bomb, go on that's it just see it being blown up and realize now that these things can Never, ever bother you again now or any time in the future as you relax more with each second that passes by and every breath that you take.

11- MIRROR TO INSTALL NEW FUTURE

Just imagine now as you relax more completely a full length mirror in your minds eye and imagine that you are standing in front of this full length mirror but rather than seeing the image of how you once were, you are now seeing the image of how you wish to be. Notice how happy and confident you feel about yourself, notice how good it feels to look in the mirror and see yourself exactly as you have on many occasions dreamed yourself to be, notice how much happier you now feel about yourself and as a result how much happier you feel around those you love and how easy it has now become to be open, honest and candid about those things which once bothered you before you became this image of beauty, happiness, confidence and contentment that you now see before you in your minds eye and then as you continue to breath deeply and regularly realizing now that this is no longer a dream, this is in fact 100% Total Reality, it is in fact your New reality and is indeed the person you have now become and will continue to be from this moment forward, as you go deeper, the better you feel the deeper you go and the deeper you go the better you will feel.

12 – PAIN & PLEASURE SUGGESTIONS

Realizing now as you relax further that from this moment forward you find and get the greatest pleasure from making yourself and others happy, from making yourself and others feel Loved, wanted, Needed and appreciated in all that they say and do and that from this moment forward you no longer need, want, crave or desire any manner of painful situation in your life as you continue to be the Confident, Happy, Healthy, Calm, Relaxed and Loving person that you have now become and will continue to be every day in every way. Making others happy makes you happy and seeing others sad makes you sad as you now live your life like a mirror and give out that which you want reflected back to you.

13 – MAJOR POST HYPNOTIC SUGGESTIONS

In a few moments time when I awaken you, everything I have suggested to you and everything that you have suggested to yourself will remain with you in every way and will grow stronger and more positive for you each second, of each minute of each hour for the rest of your life. Each and every time you consent for me to help you reenter this relaxing and beneficial state you will reenter this state with the greatest of ease and the very moment that I say **"AND SLEEP NOW"** that very moment that I say **"AND SLEEP NOW"** you will instantly and rapidly reenter this state, and each and every time you reenter this state it will be 100 times more relaxing, deeper and enjoyable for you in every way, shape and form. As you relax deeper realizing also that whenever you hear my voice on an audio cassette whether consciously or whilst asleep the effect of my positive suggestions upon you will grow stronger in every way enabling you to realize that something you once thought would be so difficult to achieve has in fact proved so ridiculously easy.

14 – AWAKEN FROM TRANCE (IF DAY) OR SEND OFF TO SLEEP IF ON TAPE AT NIGHT.

I'm now going to count from 1 to 10 and on the count of ten everything I have suggested will remain with you at a subconscious level and will grow stronger every second of each day enabling you to continue being the Confident, Happy, healthy, Relaxed, Calm and Loving individual that you have now become and will continue to be from this moment forward….

On 1, Everything I have suggested remaining with you and growing stronger in every way.

On 2, Realizing now that you will awaken in the morning with an inner warm glow of confidence, a renewed optimism to life and a more positive attitude to get things done as you now realize that you have a large inner reservoir of self-confidence, Willpower, self-esteem, Patience, Trust and Honesty within you that you can draw upon whenever necessary as an automatic reflex action.

On 3, Realizing now how much better you feel, how proud you feel about yourself for allowing yourself to come to terms with the problems you once had that no longer bother you.

0n 4, Its almost as thought every muscle in your body is now being washed with pure spring water removing all negativity from your mind, from your body and from your life forever,

0n 5, Lighter and brighter almost as though you now realize that a huge weight has now been lifted off your shoulders and you are now free to live your life happily the way you once thought may only ever be a dream, but the way which is now for you your 100% Total Personal Reality.

On 6, Normal feelings now returning to each and every muscle group in your body as everything I have suggested is now permanently burnt deep into your subconscious mind

0n 7, Realizing now that at a conscious Level only, when you awaken in a few moments time you will remember to forget and forget to remember everything that has been suggested to you, instead allowing it all to be stored to your subconscious mind who will ensure that you act upon it all as an automatic reflex action in your every day life.

On 8, Lighter and brighter now, coming on up out of it, feeling better than you have done in weeks, perhaps even in months, feeling so happy. Healthy, Calm and relaxed

As on 9, Coming on up out of it, Lighter and brighter

And on 10, Open your eyes wakey wakey rise and shine.

<u>END OF PERSONAL SESSION WHICH IS SUITABLE FOR TREATING 99% OF PHOBIAS, HABITS, PROBLEMS ETC</u>

To help you learn where you should raise and lower your voice and where you need to pause and give emphasis to certain words you would be wise to go onto You-Tube and search for "World Hypnotism Day "The Perfect

You" Hypnotherapy Quit Smoking Weight Loss Life Changing" or you can type in the direct link for the video as follows:

https://youtu.be/j5xsE4036uI

You will find that everything you see demonstrated in that video is taught somewhere within this course or can be learnt from the 47 Free Videos that you can find at this link of:

www.HypnosisWeek.com

Indeed you would also be wise to go and grab Free PDF copies of my other 3 Home Study Hypnosis Training Manuals from this link:

www.elitehypnosisbootcamp.com/freebook/

And check out our range of Home Study Video Training packages at:

www.magicalguru.co.uk   and also at **www.sellfy.com/JonathanRoyle/**

Details of our Live Personal Training Courses can be found on our sites of:

www.HtgLive.com and also **www.MagicalGuru.com**

 Well, there you have it.

<u>THE COURSE IN COMPLETE MIND THERAPY.</u>

Good Luck & Enjoy

JONATHAN ROYLE